Kathleen G. Pickett, B.Sc., is at present Senior Lecturer in the Department of Sociology in the University of Liverpool. Previously she spent two years with the Planning Department of Lancashire County Council. Her special interests are research methods and urban sociology.

David K. Boulton, B.A.(Econ.), M.A., lived for three years in Maghull, while he collected research material for this book: he specializes in urban sociology and social deviance, and is at present Head of the Sociology Department at Mather College of Education, Manchester.

Migration and social adjustment

SOCIAL RESEARCH SERIES

GENERAL EDITOR: J. B. MAYS

Other titles in this series

Industrial studies

THE DOCK WORKER
THE ATTITUDES OF STEELWORKERS
    TO TECHNICAL CHANGE
MANAGEMENT IN BRITAIN
THE CLERK IN INDUSTRY
INDUSTRIAL PARTICIPATION
COAL AND CONFLICT

Community studies

GROWING UP IN THE CITY
ON THE THRESHOLD OF DELINQUENCY
PRIESTS AND PEOPLE
EDUCATION AND THE URBAN CHILD
CHURCH AND SCHOOL
CITY LADS IN BORSTAL
WHITEGATE: AN APPROVED SCHOOL
    IN TRANSITION

Kathleen G. Pickett and
David K. Boulton
with the assistance of Norman Rankin

Migration and social adjustment
KIRKBY AND MAGHULL

WITH A FOREWORD BY JOHN BARRON MAYS

Social Research Series

LIVERPOOL UNIVERSITY PRESS 1974

Published by
LIVERPOOL UNIVERSITY PRESS
123 Grove Street, Liverpool L7 7AF

Copyright © Kathleen G. Pickett and David K. Boulton 1974

ISBN 0 85323 122 2

First published 1974

PRINTED IN GREAT BRITAIN BY
HAZELL WATSON AND VINEY LTD, AYLESBURY, BUCKS

Foreword

The two brief reports of new housing areas on Merseyside which comprise this volume continue the long-established tradition of the Department of Social Science for carrying out detailed empirical inquiries in the related fields of suburban and urban redevelopment. The first of such reports, published as long ago as 1951, *Social Aspects of a Town Development Plan*, comprised a study of the County Borough of Dudley. It was followed in 1954 by *Neighbourhood and Community* which dealt with the experiences of people living in two new housing estates, one near Liverpool, the other outside Sheffield, and the ways *inter alia* in which status and occupational differences influenced social relationships and attitudes towards other residents.

During the late 1950s and early 1960s the Crown Street research study on the social life of inner urban areas continued the tradition and focused rather more consciously on problems of planning and social organization. *Urban Redevelopment and Social Change* (1961) sought to throw factual sociological light on town-planning policy and decision-making. *Education and the Urban Child* (1962) examined the wide educational and social problems which exist in decayed inner residential areas such as the Crown Street district of Liverpool and, by inference, in other big cities.

It was hence a logical step for departmental research workers to shift their attention to the new housing estate of Kirkby where many of the original Crown Street families migrated during the decade of the 1960s. The first account of these follow-up research studies, *School of Tomorrow*,[1] tried to show what effect new opportunities provided in purpose-built comprehensive schools were having on children's educational and social lives, while the first section of the present volume looks at a variety of social topics including relations with other residents, satisfaction with housing and amenities, and various other traditional aspects of the process of adjustment to living in a new environment. David Boulton's description of similar aspects of the Maghull development area has been included for comparative purposes and because it deals with similar social issues in a more middle-class estate.

1. J. B. Mays, W. Quine, and K. Pickett, *School of Tomorrow*, Longman, 1968.

Such studies as these have always interested planners and those responsible for making policy decisions. But their very detail and concentration on selective issues has sometimes exposed them to criticism from academic sociologists, often on the grounds that they do little to advance theoretical knowledge in the field of 'urban sociology'.

These criticisms can be answered, in my view, fairly simply. In the first place we require a number of spot studies of social life in as many different kinds of urban area as we can possibly obtain if we are going to be able to appreciate the richness and variety of urban textual patterns. Every small-scale study adds its quota of factual knowledge which can be used to modify as well as to elaborate general theory. For example, had no further studies of inner working-class communities been attempted after the publication of Young's and Wilmott's *Family and Kinship in East London*, how misleading would be our ideas about apparently similar localities in Swansea or in Liverpool!

Secondly, and perhaps even more significantly, we have to recognize that urban processes are essentially dynamic in character, that people's social experiences do not remain static even in apparently stable localities. Urbanization, as Pahl reminds us in the Introduction to his *Readings in Urban Sociology*, is not a once-for-all and immutable process. He quotes Reissman to the effect that

Urbanization . . . means not only the transformation of rural, agricultural or folk society, but also the continuous change within the industrial city itself. Urbanization does not stop but continues to change the city into ever different forms.[2]

One of these forms is certainly the new housing estate and it is a fact that the experience of being obliged to be rehoused and to start a fresh life in an entirely new area is a common feature of the contemporary scene.

The search for an over-all sociological theory which would account for every change and permutation in urban life, in both the social and physical structure, such as would enable us to predict the course of future events with any degree of accuracy, is almost certainly a chimera that social scientists would do well not to follow. We have the magnificent failure of the Chicago urban ecologists as a stern warning against the pursuit of ambitious positivistic theories which seek to explain the complex and still only partly understood nature of human life and social relationships.

The *hubris* of the Chicago school lay in their determination to find some explanation of city growth which would be as objective

2. R. Pahl, *Readings in Urban Sociology*, Pergamon Press, 1968, p. 28.

and value-free as botany and ecology. They sought, that is to say, to impose what they considered to be natural scientific principles upon the human situation and habitat. They wanted to be in a position to explain why cities have grown in the way their data appeared to tell them; they wanted to be able to enunciate some general laws of urban growth and development and they hoped that, thus equipped, they could make confident predictions regarding the future. And they failed. They failed because they regarded the growth of the city as expressing an external truth about man's world. What they failed to account for, the fatal flaw in the magic crystal they created, was the essentially rational and self-determining nature of man himself. Men make cities according to their ideas of what is appropriate at a particular time and place. Cities reflect men's ideas about the social world they live in, and the difference between a medieval town, with its cluster of houses snuggled under a fortified hill, and a modern megalopolis like Los Angeles or Chicago is a measure of growth not only of technology, but, more importantly, of social and political philosophies. There are no laws, like the so-called laws of nature, to account for the transformation.

In so far as any general theory may be said to emerge from or lie behind this volume and similar earlier studies, it might be said that what above all determines the life of new estates is the structure of the wider community outside and beyond them and which in fact brought them into existence in the first place. More and more is it being borne in upon us that in a modern, comparatively affluent, technologically sophisticated, industrial society such as ours, the key to understanding the process of urban growth and change is political choice. Conversely, urban decay is attributable to absence of a plan. Choices are now possible. Decisions are made on the basis of political and moral values and in the light of expert and technically competent advice. Such values are in my judgement much more critical than financial limitations or economic considerations. There is no absolutely binding need to redevelop our outworn urban areas or to create new estates in precisely the ways we do. Tenement flat blocks, for example, are as much social as economic or architectural choices.

The socio-political structure underpins urban development policy. A stratified and élitist society redevelops its obsolete parts in terms of its present assumptions. Choices are differentially available. Better-off people can to some extent choose their house and select their neighbourhood. Indeed one of the crucial differences between people seems to be the ability to exercise choice between private and corporation housing. It is clear, too, from the evidence in this volume that choice also influences residents' satisfaction with their new area.

Furthermore, one of the factors which assists choice and promotes satisfaction is the availability not only of a suitable house but of a rewarding occupation, either in terms of money earned or in terms of job satisfaction.

We return then to the political and economic base of society. The most successful migrants are those people who want to move, are occupationally motivated, and have some choice about where they go and regarding the kind of house in which to establish their home. Hence the similarity of experience and aspiration on the part of the residents of Maghull makes for a degree of homogeneity which nevertheless does not approach the classic sociological concept of a community.

The general pragmatism of English tradition invades and influences urban and suburban planning as all other departments of our national life. This is something that social scientists must take cognizance of in formulating explanatory theories. Life in the new areas such as Kirkby is part gain, part loss. Probably in the long term the gains will greatly outstrip present losses. The evolution of a more equal society, whether in education, occupational opportunity, environmental amenity or house satisfaction seems to be steadily under way. To the extent that research workers have been able to monitor relevant aspects of this evolutionary process they are clearly contributing to future social history. By highlighting social problems and sore spots they almost certainly help to speed up the social evolutionary process itself.

In presenting these researches in monograph form I would like to pay tribute to various colleagues who have given assistance during the course of the field work and analysis. Norman Rankin worked closely with me in the initial study of Kirkby and he was the author of the first short report on the inquiry, an article in the *Sociological Review*, volume xi, no. 3 (1963), 'Social adjustment in a north west New Town'. Various other members of the department helped in carrying out the early field work and Miss Betty Gittus gave valuable statistical advice, both at this and at later stages of the inquiry. We are grateful to her for allowing us to make use of certain hitherto unpublished data in the present book. We would also like to record our gratitude to Mr G. Mercer, Chief Planning Officer, Trafford, for information in Chapter 4, and to Mr J. W. Davies of Lancashire County Council Educational Department for help on the chapter on leisure.

Department of Sociology   J. B. MAYS
The University of Liverpool

Contents

Appendices

List of tables

List of maps

CHAPTER 1

Introduction

One of the most important ecological tendencies of recent years has been the drift of urban populations outwards from the city centre to the suburbs. Until the redevelopment of 'inner cities' began on any large scale a monopoly of new housing development took place in new suburbs, which were built in previously undeveloped areas surrounding cities and towns. Movement of population to the suburbs has resulted in a relative depopulation of the central city area, and often also in a decrease in the population of the city since many recent suburbs, though economically and socially within the sphere of influence of the parent city, have been built beyond the city's administrative boundaries.

This book brings together two studies carried out in areas just outside the Merseyside conurbation; both are concerned with the social effects of migration in different settings though in a narrow geographical context (Map 1, p. 2). Kirkby is separated from the Liverpool boundary by only two miles. It developed from an old-established agricultural parish in West Lancashire Rural District with a population of 3,000 in 1951 to an Urban District of 34,000 residents in 1958. Maghull, five miles from the Liverpool boundary, four miles west of Kirkby, and still within West Lancashire Rural District, developed in Victorian times as a commuter suburb on the railway line to Liverpool, but large-scale housing development has taken place mainly in the last twenty years.

The study of Kirkby, an estate built by Liverpool Corporation to house Liverpool people, concerns the public sector answer to rehousing. The study of Maghull concentrates on the private sector. Its private housing is available on the market not only to Liverpool people but also to people from wider afield who have moved into the Merseyside area. In Maghull therefore there are people whose traditions are not those of Liverpool, but to all but a limited extent both areas may be seen to serve the same function of supplying accommodation which the city is no longer able to provide within its boundaries; and both areas depend upon Liverpool for their economic prosperity since a high proportion of their residents find employment there. Liverpool's social influence also spreads to these

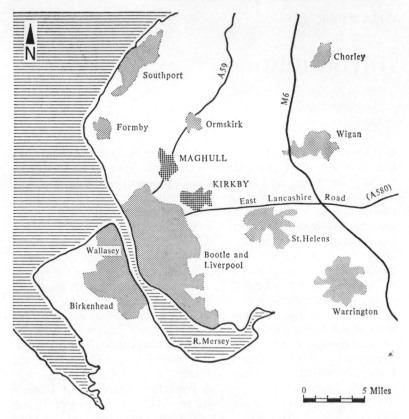

Map 1. Showing the relationship of Kirkby and Maghull to other areas of west Lancashire.

areas by way of family and friendship ties and facilities for entertainment and association.

Since 1945 the city has made a sustained effort to break away from dependence upon a very limited number of industries, a feature which before the Second World War resulted in its being one of the hardest hit areas during periods of depression. Liverpool's early prosperity and growth were largely based upon shipping and the textile trade, and both of these industries have been in a serious decline since before the war. From the 1950s onwards new growth industries have been attracted to Liverpool and these appear to be reducing the movement to the Midlands and south of some of the region's highly skilled and trained workers, a movement which has been taking place over many years. In addition a growing movement northwards from the south and Midlands has been evident, resulting between 1965 and 1966 in a net gain to the local authorities peripheral to the Merseyside conurbation.[1] Kirkby and Maghull are part of this changing aspect of Merseyside. Kirkby town is situated adjacent to a thriving industrial estate and provides a growing number of employees for the new industries. Maghull attracts migrants from outside the region as well as those whose home is Merseyside, many of whom owe their greater affluence to the region's increasing prosperity.

These two reports are largely concerned with people's attitudes to their environment in the form of the house or flat they live in and the area in which it is located. Well over half the people of Maghull interviewed in the 1967 survey had lived in Liverpool during their youth and all these people expressed satisfaction with their home. In the Kirkby study, on the other hand, about one-third of those interviewed in 1961 expressed a positive wish to move away from the town, and a further smaller proportion said that they would only want to stay subject to some change in their accommodation.

It appears from these studies that the people in Maghull have adapted more easily and quickly to their new environment than have the people of Kirkby; and while many critics of public sector development have attributed this failure to adapt to the lack of entertainment facilities, community centres, and other aspects of material culture, the Maghull study seems to show that people in private housing have avoided the trauma of resettlement despite the lack of these facilities. This suggests that factors other than physical defects on new estates are at work, and a likely explanation may be that people buying houses in the private sector have been able to meet choices and demands which the people in the public sector have not been able to satisfy.

H. J. Gans suggests that ecological explanations of social life are not satisfactory when people are able to make choices, and continues:

If the supply of housing and of neighbourhoods is such that alternatives are available, however, people will make choices, and if the housing market is responsive, they can even make and satisfy explicit demands.[2]

There is, however, no such regular pattern in the Liverpool housing market. The distinction between private and public housing means that for an individual looking for a new house or neighbourhood the

1. See K. G. Pickett, 'Migration in the Merseyside area', in *Merseyside Social and Economic Studies*, ed. R. Lawton and C. Cunningham, Longman, 1970, chapter 5.

2. H. J. Gans, 'Urbanism and suburbanism as ways of life: a re-valuation of definitions', reprinted in *Readings in Urban Sociology*, ed. R. E. Pahl, 1968, p.110.

choice is limited by the ability to buy. In this sense it is constraint rather than choice which controls migration in the first place.

For the resident from downtown Liverpool, for instance, the improved physical conditions of the Kirkby estate may represent an initial satisfaction of a demand for a better standard of housing. He may have been able to indicate a choice for the area he is moved to, but in this respect constraints imposed by the local authority's housing list deny him all but a modicum of effective choice. On the other hand the private house buyer in Maghull will argue that he was able to exercise a much more effective choice; but in fact constraints imposed by the size of the mortgage he was able to obtain and by the limited availability of housing in the lower price range mean that in reality he is only marginally more free to choose than the person who lives in Kirkby.

One important factor in considering adjustment to migration may well be the question of whether the person involved *feels* that he has exercised choice rather than whether or not he has actually done so. Gans suggests that

Choices and demands do not develop independently or at random; they are functions of the roles people play in the social system. These can best be understood in terms of the characteristics of the people involved ... Although many characteristics affect the choices and demands people make with respect to housing and neighbourhoods, the most important ones seem to be *class* in all its economic, social and cultural ramifications —and *life-cycle stage*.[3]

Maghull, with its remarkable homogeneity of life styles, appears to be the home of either 'status assenting' middle-class or 'status dissenting'[4] working-class people. Its residents have similar demands in relation to house choice, neighbourhood, and way of life, and adjustment for the majority is no problem since they have satisfied their demands.

The Kirkby study, and the preceding study of the Crown Street area of Liverpool[5] from which many of the town's residents originated, suggest that much of the motivation for the move to Kirkby resulted from a desire for environmental change and that this was especially strong among young married couples. However, a considerable number in Kirkby had not wanted to move there. Since these people began living in Kirkby without having satisfied any of

3. Ibid., p. 111.

4. These terms, which were first introduced by J. M. Mogey in *Family and Neighbourhood*, Oxford University Press, 1956, have been developed by J. Klein in *Samples from English Cultures*, Routledge and Kegan Paul, 1966, vol. 1, pp. 238–46.

5. C. Vereker, J. B. Mays, E. Gittus, and M. Broady, *Urban Redevelopment and Social Change*, Liverpool University Press, 1961.

their demands, problems of adjustment among them would not be surprising. Length of residence appears to be an important factor in such adjustment: information from long-established local authority estates suggests that over time many people become reconciled to a move without apparent choice, while those unable to do so move away, some back to the city centre, others in better circumstances to a suburban home of their own. Long-term acceptance of Kirkby appears to depend less upon the physical advantages, which are important in the short term, than upon the establishment of social contacts.

The situation in Kirkby described in the following pages is now largely a historical one. Delay in publication has been a result of a normal hazard for departmental research, in that those who planned and carried out the survey left before the data were fully available.[6] Nevertheless it is hoped that at a time when a decision has been reached to proceed with a third Lancashire New Town at Leyland and Chorley, there will be some interest in an early attempt to establish a new town without the advantages of independence provided by 'New Town' designation.

During the intervening years Maghull has developed, and it may well be that among its present residents are a number who were living in Kirkby when the Kirkby survey was carried out. Maghull and estates like it today provide a goal for those rejecting the implications of city terrace or corporation tenancy—the new working-class status dissenters whose circumstances have improved sufficiently to allow their aspirations to be translated into action.

6. A preliminary report on Kirkby, entitled 'Social adjustment in a north west New Town', was written by N. Rankin and published in the *Sociological Review*, xi, 3 (1963).

I KIRKBY

CHAPTER 2

Kirkby, the town

From the road southwards to Kirkby across the fertile west Lancashire plain, tall concrete blocks of flats appear suddenly on the horizon. Approached from this direction, the town rises out of farming country where Lancashire's rural architecture is characteri stically dour rectangular, grey-stone-walled, and slate-roofed; but over the years it has acquired some charm, and its sturdiness is well-suited to a countryside giving little shelter from prevailing westerly winds sweeping in from the sea. Kirkby architecture, on the other hand, is free from local influence and entirely characteristic of the mid-twentieth-century housing estate, functional and concrete-dominated. In the particular circumstances of the time, however, Kirkby's form of construction appears inevitable for the town was designed to house the maximum possible number of people in housing need in the least possible time using, under government insistence, a minimum of the high-quality agricultural land on which it was built.

In pre-war years Liverpool had serious housing problems, and plans for rebuilding its slum areas were made in the 1930s. Some of the redevelopment of these years, mainly in the form of flats and tenements (blocks of five or six storeys) attracted wide attention both for design and layout: they were considered by many to be in the forefront of municipal housing. The war put an end to this and increased the problem, for bombing in the central areas destroyed many houses, leaving large numbers homeless or sharing accommodation in even worse conditions. This urgent and serious situation required immediate attention after the war, and it was obvious that rebuilding within the areas of the city requiring redevelopment would be too slow and in any case of insufficient size to meet the need. Plans were therefore made to construct what were described as 'comprehensive self-contained housing estates' on the periphery of the city, including some outside its boundaries.

Kirkby, seven miles from the centre of Liverpool, is the largest of these estates, its situation chosen because there was already in existence there a successful trading estate owned by the Corporation which could provide employment for new residents. There was suitable building land nearby owned by Lancashire County Council,

who were ready to co-operate in its development. The County
Council, as the statutory planning authority, drew up the Development Plan for Kirkby in 1950, which proposed an eventual community of 40,000 people who would move in over a period of fifteen
years. Under pressure from Liverpool, however, this was modified
to 50,000 people within six years, a programme of exceptional size
which was in the event virtually adhered to.

The design of the town followed New Town lines and the density
of dwellings required was achieved largely by a high proportion of
flat blocks. These are of a repetitive and monotonous character,
their layout concerned more with density figures than visual interest
and variety. Nevertheless the complete formlessness of many
smaller estates was avoided. The town centre, under construction
at the time of the survey, is of some size, and besides shops and
banks includes a lively market and market-place, library, official
buildings, a large club, and a community centre with adjacent
offices dealing with community organizations.

The town in 1961 was divided into three neighbourhoods, Southdene, Northwood, and Westvale (Map 2, p. 11), the last quite separate
from the other two. Shops, primary schools, and pubs are clustered
at several neighbourhood centres. While the primary schools serve
the neighbourhoods in which they are located, the four comprehensive schools, two county and two Roman Catholic, take children
from the town as a whole.

The estate was based on a small agricultural parish with a population in 1951 of 3,000. As a result of the nearby industrial development, services of considerable usefulness already existed—water,
electricity, and gas supplies, new main roads and public transport.
The first dwellings were occupied in 1952 and construction of houses
proceeded rapidly, being virtually completed by 1959. As is usual in
municipal estate development, non-housing construction was mainly
left until this was done. In 1958 Kirkby became an Urban District,
and by 1966 it was estimated that the population had reached 60,000.[1]

Lancashire has throughout been the planning authority for Kirkby
and the provider of 'county' services. Liverpool had intended that,
like another of its large-scale developments at Speke, Kirkby should
be included within the boundaries of the city by means of a statutory
extension, but this was successfully opposed by Lancashire. Given
the relatively greater demands on Liverpool's municipal financial
resources and the cultural problems posed by the city, Lancashire
seemed more likely to be an effective provider of upper-tier local
government services at Kirkby than Liverpool would have been;

1. The 1966 Sample Census gives a total population of 55,000 but this is
believed to be understated.

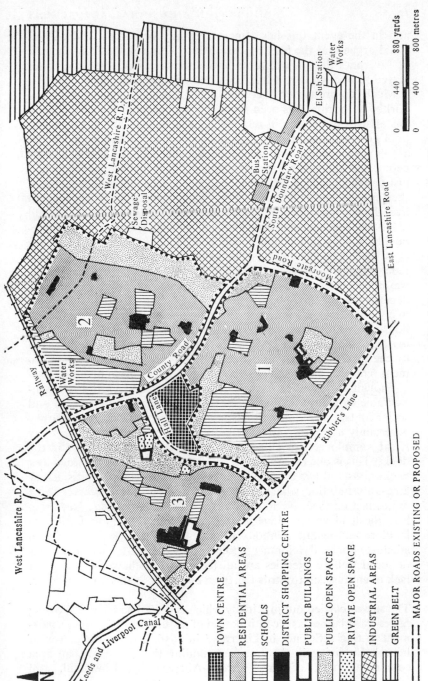

N

West Lancashire R.D.

Leeds and Liverpool Canal

Railway

Water Works

West Lancashire R.D.

Sewage Disposal

Bus Station

El.Sub.Station

Water Works

South Boundary Road

Moorgate Road

County Road

Hall Lane

Ribbler's Lane

East Lancashire Road

2

1

3

0   440   880 yards
0   400   800 metres

TOWN CENTRE

RESIDENTIAL AREAS

SCHOOLS

DISTRICT SHOPPING CENTRE

PUBLIC BUILDINGS

PUBLIC OPEN SPACE

PRIVATE OPEN SPACE

INDUSTRIAL AREAS

GREEN BELT

MAJOR ROADS EXISTING OR PROPOSED

Map 2. Kirkby, showing the neighbourhoods 1. Southdene, 2. Northwood, and 3. Westvale.

and in the event this has almost certainly been true. Indeed one could argue that the Speke estate, which was isolated from the rest of Liverpool though within its boundaries, would have been better served if, like Kirkby, it had been retained in Lancashire.

Much co-ordination between the Liverpool, Lancashire, and Kirkby authorities has been necessary and some of the conflict that has arisen can be seen in retrospect to have been inevitable. Liverpool's chief concern has been to house families in need, to reduce by a small proportion her enormous housing list. To many Kirkby people, on the other hand, it appeared that the Corporation had just put them 'over the border' with the minimum consideration of their preference for the area or type of home in which they were to live, the Corporation's only real interest being the profit they could make on their undertaking. The rent subsidy received from Liverpool by Kirkby households is, however, substantial, in spite of heavy calls on corporation funds for other housing schemes including redevelopment in the city. Nevertheless, dislike of the Corporation was often expressed strongly by Kirkby residents, who resented their dependence on an absentee landlord. Such difficulties, arising in many similar situations over the country, suggest that large-scale housing developments by corporations, such as that in Kirkby or, in a very different area, Dagenham, might be more suitably managed by the type of commission which administers New Town development schemes, once the constructional stage has been completed.

Though the distance from Kirkby to central Liverpool is inconsiderable by many standards, Kirkby is regarded in its regional and social context as requiring too long a journey to work. The journey is certainly a great deal longer than that previously made by many Kirkby employees travelling between the centre of the city and the docks. This is one reason why Kirkby has always been regarded as a backwoods and has become a stereotype of a socially unsatisfactory area—a reputation which often seems to a detached observer to be unjustified or excessive in the face of ascertainable facts. Nevertheless, the tendency for Liverpool Corporation to confine itself to a landlord-and-tenant relationship, the failure to develop early an adequate social development policy, and the inadequate resources of social welfare agencies are all factors which have encouraged a lack of enthusiasm towards the town among residents and outsiders.

The survey carried out in Kirkby which is described in the following pages was planned as a continuation of a study made by the Department of Social Science in Liverpool in 1956. This was a survey of households living in the area surrounding the University, an area comprising most of three wards—Abercromby, Low Hill, and

Smithdown—which were considered to be representative of a blighted inner residential urban zone requiring major redevelopment or rehabilitation. A comprehensive report on this area—the 'Crown Street area'—has been published.[2]

In the nineteenth century much of this area, in particular parts of Abercromby ward, housed prosperous city business men. It was a desirable area: at this point the land rises quite steeply from the Mersey and at its summit gives fine views over the river to Cheshire and the Welsh hills beyond. Many of the large and once elegant Regency buildings still stand, but for the most part they have deteriorated structurally and are now valued only for their convenience for conversion into flats or rooms. Other parts of the area contain rows of terrace houses in varying conditions, mostly built during the later part of the nineteenth century, intermingled with small factories and workshops. During the 1930s some corporation flats were put up, and a number of corporation houses were erected shortly after the last war, but apart from these and university buildings very little construction has taken place in recent years. Although some of the flat conversions are good, most of the property is in poor condition, varying from 'drab respectability' to 'squalid poverty',[3] and much of it is scheduled for early demolition. In the meantime it houses many families and individuals for whom it is a problem to find suitable housing which they can afford. Young couples with children whose husbands are frequently unemployed or on casual work and the mobile unattached find in this locality a place where relatively cheap furnished accommodation is available from landlords, who are not concerned with the number or nationality of the people they house so long as the rent is paid, nor about the condition of the property they let out.

The 1956 survey took account of the physical condition of the area and also of the social background of its residents. Against this it considered the attitude of residents to the locality and their desire for change. As the survey was being made, it was found that some families were already being moved away by the Corporation, many to its estate at Kirkby. This movement was to continue, and by 1959 some 700 families had moved from 'Crown Street' to Kirkby. It seemed appropriate, therefore, to make an attempt to discover what changes this migration had made in the lives of the rehoused families and what were their attitudes to the change.

In 1960, when the Kirkby survey was planned, the population of the town was 51,300. Liverpool Corporation's housing lists gave the addresses of former Crown Street residents now in Kirkby and from these a random sample of households was selected; in this report

2. Vereker, et al., Urban Redevelopment and Social Change.   3. Ibid., p. 15.

this sample is called the 'Crown Street sample'. In order to compare the reactions of this group of families with those on the estate generally, a 2 per cent sample of addresses of all Kirkby households was obtained from the electoral register. Only about 8 per cent of these had originally lived in Crown Street and it is from this latter sample, the 'General sample', that any generalizations concerning the estate may be made. For the General sample, 196 addresses were selected using a sampling fraction of 1 in 50 and a random starting point. The response rate was 93 per cent, providing a total of 183 households interviewed. The Crown Street sample gave a similar response rate (94 per cent), resulting in a total of 108 households interviewed.

Many of the questions asked in the 1956 Crown Street survey were included in the Kirkby schedule, which is reproduced in Appendix E. Those sections concerned with basic socio-economic information, kinship, membership of churches and organizations, and attitudes towards their present dwelling and locality were much the same in both schedules. The Kirkby schedule was extended, however, to include questions on informal interaction and attitudes towards neighbours, social organizations, and other local amenities. Interviews were with either the head of household, with very few exceptions a married man, or the wife of the head. No other member of the household was accepted as respondent. Though a substantial amount of interviewing took place in the evenings the majority of visits were made during the day; since most men are not at home during the day this resulted in considerably more women than men being interviewed. Comparisons between their responses have been widely made and show negligible differences.

There were seven interviewers, all either members of staff of the Department of Social Science or associated with the Department. Households were visited without notice and where possible the interview was conducted at the time, though frequently a later appointment was arranged. The data collected were coded and recorded on punched cards in the Department. Separate analyses have been made for the two samples.

Where it has seemed appropriate, a chi-squared test of significance has been made. Criticisms of the use of this test[4] have not been considered substantial enough to outweigh its advantages. Where a 'significant' difference has been noted in the test, this infers that the probability of such a difference occurring by chance is less than 5 per cent.

CHAPTER 3

The Kirkby household

Kirkby is a young town, not only in relation to years of construction but also in the age structure of its residents. In New Towns this is characteristically skewed towards the younger groups, and Kirkby displays such a tendency to a marked degree. It is from this that its public image and reputation are largely derived.

Half the members of households selected for interview were under 15 years of age, and only 3 per cent were 60 years old or more. This coincides closely with 1961 Census figures for Kirkby. In comparison, only a quarter of the population of Liverpool in 1961[1] was under 15 years old and 15 per cent were 60 or older; Crown Street households in 1956 displayed similar proportions. In England and Wales generally in 1961 the proportions were 23 per cent under 15 and 18 per cent aged 60 or more. Kirkby's age structure may be compared with the New Towns of Harlow and Crawley, where in 1961 37 per cent and 34 per cent of their population respectively was under 15 years of age, and 5 per cent and 7 per cent respectively aged 60 and over (Table 1).

More than half of the General sample and two-thirds of the Crown Street sample households had obtained houses in Kirkby

TABLE 1

*Age structure of Kirkby residents compared with the
Crown Street area, Liverpool C.B., Harlow U.D.,
and Crawley U.D.*

| Age group | Kirkby survey | | | | | |
	General sample	Crown St. sample	Crown St. 1956	L'pool 1961	Harlow 1961	Crawley 1961
	%	%	%	%	%	%
0–4	18	16	10	9	15	13
5–14	32	35	20	17	22	21
15–20	7	8	10	9	5	5
21–59	41	38	48	50	53	54
60 and over	3	3	12	15	5	7

1. 1961 Sample Census data.

because they were in urgent need of suitable accommodation and as a result their names had been placed at the top of Liverpool Corporation's housing list. Kirkby was built at a time when this list was particularly long, and with few exceptions only families in the highest priority of housing need or those whose houses were about to be demolished to allow redevelopment in the city were eligible for a new corporation dwelling.

The composition of the Kirkby household, therefore, generally adds up to that typically associated with new public authority housing projects: a high proportion of two-generation households of young parents and children of school age or less. Well over half the heads of household of both samples were under 40 years old at the time of the survey, compared with 30 per cent in Crown Street in 1956 (Table 2). All but about 15 per cent of the households contained

TABLE 2

Age of heads of household, Kirkby and the 1956 Crown Street area

	Kirkby survey		
Age group	General sample	Crown St. sample	Crown St. 1956
	%	%	%
Less than 20	1	—	—
20–29	14	12	10
30–39	45	44	20
40–49	28	19	22
50–59	8	12	19
60–64	2	6	8
65 and over	2	6	21
No. of households	183	108	574

two generations. Single generation households were a very small minority, and those with three generations even smaller (Table 26, Appendix A). Such young families are very liable to be affected by bad housing conditions when their resources are few and, therefore, are most likely to qualify for rehousing by the local authority. This is also the type of household in which in 1956 the desire to move away from the Crown Street area was most often expressed.

Records of Liverpool Corporation's Housing Department confirm that the main basis for a tenancy in Kirkby was housing need and not redevelopment (Table 27, Appendix A). Liverpool residents described as in 'housing need' are largely those on the Corporation's waiting list for housing whose claim for rehousing is based on their inability to obtain suitable accommodation for themselves because there are young children in the household and income is limited. The description could also relate at times to families living within areas or in individual properties scheduled for demolition because of their poor condition, but a substantial number of Kirkby residents came from areas which could not be designated 'slums'. Most of those moving for this reason, however, were from the Crown Street area or neighbouring districts.

Of the residents who had not obtained tenancies for either of these reasons, a high proportion had moved to Kirkby through exchanging their house. Mainly these were from other local authority housing estates, but a few were from other parts of Kirkby itself. The proportion rehoused for medical reasons was small, and there was no evidence from the interviews conducted at Kirkby that those given tenancies for this reason were grouped together because of a block allocation at a particular time, as occurred on a Glasgow housing estate. In addition there were a small number of 'nominated tenants', housed through a procedure whereby tenants in privately rented property may be provided with a dwelling by Liverpool Corporation, which then has the right to nominate a tenant from the housing list for the vacated private accommodation. Occasional tenancies were also granted to key workers whose availability was regarded as essential for their particular firms on the industrial estate.

A family obtaining a tenancy through priority on the Corporation's housing list, therefore, had usually been living in overcrowded conditions; and significantly more of the Crown Street than the General sample households were rehoused on this basis. The 1956 Crown Street survey found that nearly a quarter of households living in Abercromby ward, one of the three wards in the area, occupied only one room, and Census data show that this was the case in 1961 (Table 28, Appendix A). The position was much less serious in Low Hill and Smithdown wards, where only 3 per cent and 1 per cent of households respectively lived in this condition; this is reflected in the smaller proportion of previous residents of these wards in Kirkby. An additional indication of previous overcrowding is given by the fact that 42 per cent of the General and 63 per cent of the Crown Street sample stated that they had previously occupied accommodation which contained two or more households. A third of those sharing in Crown Street had, in fact, shared with four or more households.

More than half the Crown Street households previously lived in Abercromby ward, the part of the Crown Street area containing many large houses which were once the homes of wealthy Liverpool citizens and now form part of a decaying area where large numbers of flats and rooms of varying standards of construction and cleanliness may be found. Only a small proportion of the General sample, however, had previously lived anywhere in the Crown Street area, though over half were from inner Liverpool (Table 3). Another third were from outer districts, often from pockets of old, poor housing in suburbs which were once small townships in their own right.

TABLE 3

Previous place of residence of Kirkby households

Previous place of residence	General sample		Crown St. sample	
	No.	%	No.	%
Abercromby ward	9	5	57	53
Low Hill ward	4	2	29	27
Smithdown ward	2	1	22	20
Total Crown St. district	15	8	108	100
Neighbouring wards	28	15	—	—
Other parts inner Liverpool	63	34	—	—
Total inner Liverpool*	106	58	108	100
Total outer Liverpool†	57	31	—	—
Total Liverpool	163	89	108	100
Other parts Merseyside	8	4	—	—
Other parts U.K.	10	5	—	—
Not known	2	1	—	—
Total all groups	183	100	108	100

* 1951 Census sub-divisions ia, iia, iib.
† 1951 Census sub-divisions iic, iiia, iiib.

The large size of intake families was one factor accounting for the youthfulness of the town, and another was the unusually high birth rate which prevailed among these families. In 1960 Kirkby's crude birth rate was 28·7 per 1,000 compared with 17·2 in England and Wales, 21·2 in Liverpool, and 28·2 in Harlow. It had by then declined from its peak of 30·6 in 1958, and this downward trend appears to be continuing.[2] Kirkby's high birth rate is often attributed to the unusually high proportion of Roman Catholics among the population, for more than half the households in the survey were either wholly or in part of this denomination. However, there is no evidence that Roman Catholic families in Kirkby were larger than others (Table 4). Under the particular circumstances of selection for tenancy it would, of course, be impossible to examine the relative

2. By 1966 it had declined to 18·1 (area compatability factor = 0·97).

TABLE 4

Size of Kirkby households by denomination

	No. of children									
	General sample					Crown St. sample				
Denomination	0	1–3	4–5	6 and over	Total	0	1–3	4–5	6 and over	Total
	%	%	%	%	%	%	%	%	%	%
Roman Catholic	3	25	10	3	41	5	19	10	8	42
Part Roman Catholic	—	8	4	2	14	0	8	8	4	20
Other	5	20	11	1	37	8	12	6	5	31
Not known	1	4	2	1	8	—	5	1	1	7
Total	9	57	27	7	100	13	44	25	18	100

size of Roman Catholic families generally. It is certainly true to say that in the area from which a high proportion of the families have come, there is a strong tendency towards large families whether Roman Catholic or not. Household size did not differ significantly between the two samples, although there was a tendency for the Crown Street sample to contain a greater number with seven or more members (Table 29, Appendix A). Slightly more than half the households in both samples contained five persons or more.

About three-quarters of all Kirkby households consisted of married heads with unmarried children. There were also a small number of widowed or divorced heads with unmarried children, but very few with no children at all—a distribution very different from that found in the Crown Street area in 1956 (Table 5). There, in just over half the households all children were unmarried while about a quarter contained no children. Very few childless Kirkby households included relatives of the head: where this did occur the head was unmarried. Many more such households occurred in Crown Street, but of course those would not usually qualify for a corporation tenancy.

Nearly all Kirkby residents had previously lived in Liverpool— as a condition of tenancy. Those who had not would have obtained their tenancy under special circumstances, such as that the head was a key worker at one of the local factories. Few suburbs of Liverpool can claim occupants more attached to the city by birth-place and up-bringing than can Kirkby: nearly three-quarters of husbands and wives in the General sample and two-thirds in the

TABLE 5

*Household composition of Kirkby households and
1956 Crown Street area households*

	Kirkby survey		
Type of household (*excluding non-relatives*)	*General sample*	*Crown St. sample*	*Crown St. 1956*
	%	%	%
Households without children:			
Single head living alone	—	2	6
Single head with relative(s)	1	1	3
Others*	9	9	27
Households with children:			
All children unmarried	77	82	55
Some children unmarried	7	4	5
Children and relatives	6	2	5

* Includes widowed, divorced or separated heads, and head and wife.

Crown Street sample were born in Liverpool (Table 30, Appendix A). Of the latter, over half were born in the Crown Street area itself or neighbouring wards, and must with few exceptions have lived all their lives in this part of Liverpool before moving to Kirkby. This may be compared with Crown Street residents in the 1956 survey where one-third of the heads and one-quarter of their wives were born in this area. A very small number from the Crown Street sample were born in Eire, and only one head of household from each sample came from Northern Ireland.

There is a very clear tendency for husbands and wives to belong to the same general area. In both samples nearly half of those husbands born in inner Liverpool[3] had wives also born in this area, while in an additional 16 per cent of General and 12 per cent of Crown Street households both partners were born in some part of Liverpool (Table 31, Appendix A). A very high proportion of heads and their wives had lived in the city all their lives before moving to Kirkby (Table 32, Appendix A). Length of residence in the city is taken into account when corporation tenancies are allocated, so that such people are likely to be relatively well represented.

Substantially more Kirkby households were living in flats after their move than before (Table 33, Appendix A), but although most exchanged accommodation was from tenements,[4] no respondent who had previously lived in this type of dwelling moved by exchange to a flat in Kirkby. In all only four exchanges had been made to flats,

3. 1951 Census sub-divisions ia, iia, and iib.
4. City flats built by the Corporation in the 1930s.

and the remainder were to houses; there is no doubt that block flats are generally an unpopular type of accommodation and usually only taken when there is no other choice available. The most commonly heard complaint from flat dwellers themselves was of poor insulation and noise. It was alleged that conversation in neighbouring flats could be overheard, that it was not even possible to distinguish between knocks on the outer doors, and that plumbing noise was obtrusive. Those on the ground floor also complained that people walking past would bang on their windows (of larger than usual Kirkby size) or look in, often 'watching the TV with them'. Noise was regarded as the main problem associated with living in flats on a number of estates surveyed by the Ministry of Housing and Local Government in 1964,[5] and it was noted in this survey that London's multi-storey dwellings are better insulated than those in Liverpool. Noise from neighbours within the same building appears to be a good deal more disturbing than outdoor noise, and can cause strain to mothers of young children who try to keep them quiet.

Kirkby flat-dwellers were generally regarded, and regarded themselves, as lower in status than those living in houses. One respondent, who was a flat-dweller himself, went so far as to suggest that others in the block were 'virtually sub-human'. The social division, however ill-founded, was a real one. House-dwellers regarded themselves as fortunate and flat-dwellers unlucky, unable to get away by exchange and therefore compelled to remain in housing circumstances which involved considerable psychological stress for many. Significantly more Crown Street households previously living in rooms moved to a Kirkby flat; the flat may have been accepted as the lesser of two evils, perhaps with the hope of a transfer to a house later. There was also in earlier years some tendency for flats to have lower rentals than houses of comparable capacity, and this may have made them more acceptable to lower-paid workers.

Kirkby rents tended to be substantially higher than those previously paid by respondents, though former rents varied considerably according to whether accommodation was furnished or not. At the time of the Crown Street survey the Rent Restriction Act was in operation, and more than half the households in that survey paid less than 15s. a week (Table 34, Appendix A). Only sporadic complaints relating to increased payment for rent on moving were heard in Kirkby, and although recent rent increases were criticized, these criticisms also occurred less often than might have been expected; probably the additional space provided and the amenities available were taken into account. One of the few comments made at all often

5. *Families Living at High Density*, M.O.H.L.G., 1964.

was that rents for flats were high in proportion to those for houses. Rents may, in fact, be reduced by the Corporation in cases of need, but this service is not generally advertised and no reference was made to it by respondents.

Evidence from the survey does not suggest that differences in socio-economic structure are related either to the type of house occupied in Kirkby, or to the basis for rehousing, except that significantly more old-age pensioners lived in small terrace houses. As a result of Liverpool Corporation's policy, families in flats tended to be of smaller size than those in houses and with few young children, but there were exceptions, such as one family with seven children whose mother complained that her neighbour was 'always knocking' because of the noise.

Southdene was the first of the three Kirkby neighbourhoods to be built, followed by Westvale, with Northwood a little later (Table 35, Appendix A). Because of the sequence of construction the population of Northwood tends to be the youngest of the three, and that of Southdene the oldest. At the time of the survey a significantly higher proportion of families in Northwood contained children under four years old than those of other neighbourhoods, and a higher proportion of families in Southdene contained children of school age. This difference in age structure may in part account for the preferences given by residents for different neighbourhoods. A number of respondents asserted that Southdene was the best part of the estate—'more select' was a typical comment—while Northwood and Westvale were less popular and often described as 'rowdy', or as one housewife said: 'Northwood and Westvale seem to be lower classes.'

It did not appear from the General sample that households from any particular area had been allocated to one neighbourhood rather than another, but there are significantly more semi-skilled and unskilled workers in Westvale. Nearly all tenants in this neighbourhood were rehoused on the basis of housing need or demolition, and significantly fewer on other bases such as exchange than in Southdene or Northwood. Westvale, in fact, drew the most disapproving comments of all from residents of other neighbourhoods, such as 'In Westvale all the people are from terrible districts, from what I have heard', and 'In Westvale people are very rowdy—cleared a slum and made a slum.'

Half the sample households had arrived in Kirkby by 1956 and all except four of the remaining half had moved in by 1959. Households in the Crown Street sample which had moved out since the end of 1959 were not followed up, and the household which had taken its place was not interviewed. This did not apply to the General sample where households were interviewed whatever their date of arrival. Unfortunately official records did not provide adequate information on the movement of families out of Kirkby, for this would have been of considerable interest.

The Kirkby age structure and household composition create many problems for the future. First, a possible flooding of the local labour market may occur as the children reach school-leaving age, which will be particularly serious if unskilled work is sought. Even where apprenticeships are required difficulties arise: this was found in Harlow where in a similar situation the number of school leavers trebled in eleven years. Kirkby schools seem very conscious of the danger and the consequent need to persuade their pupils to remain at school[6] and to acquire a skill of some kind, for only if this is done can a new centre of long-term unemployment be avoided. A second possible consequence may be an excess of school places in the future, though there is at present plenty of room for a substantial reduction in class size.

A third problem most likely to arise is that the homes which are now so well filled and often overcrowded will eventually contain in most cases only the two parents with perhaps an occasional un-married child or solitary relative. A large proportion of Kirkby houses will almost certainly be under-occupied while at the same time there will be a shortage of homes for Liverpool families still in need, as well as those displaced as redevelopment gets under way. New homes will also be required for the next generation of Kirkby families who will need accommodation in their turn. This unsuit-able distribution of housing space is not likely to be easily adjusted. Turner[7] points out that the spread of intake over a long period will reduce abnormalities of structure such as are found in Kirkby, which necessarily give rise to severe difficulties in the future, and that given such a situation areas should be left aside for future growth. It would then not be necessary for the children to move away, leaving an ageing population.

In the original Kirkby Development Plan no provision was made for future requirements by second generation Kirkby families. Recently the urban district has been able to acquire some land and is putting up houses specifically for this purpose. Nevertheless, the majority of Kirkby children who marry must move back to Liver-pool to find somewhere to live, and can only return to a Kirkby dwelling by qualifying for a place on the city's housing list. It would seem that there might be a case for local houses of a smaller size,

6. See J. B. Mays, W. Quine, and K. Pickett, *School of Tomorrow*, Longman, 1968, for an account of one Kirkby comprehensive school.
7. R. Turner, *Expanding Towns*, A.T.P.I. thesis (Manchester), 1959.

which would encourage exchanges between parents whose children had left them, and a growing young family. This would be more popular than a move over a distance to an unfamiliar area, which would rarely be made voluntarily unless there were strong financial inducements. There is so far no precedent for such exchanges, and whether or not they will ever be introduced depends on how urgent the future situation turns out to be. Nevertheless, one day the Kirkby streets will no longer be overflowing with young children, and the town, now orientated to its juvenile population, will need to consider the requirements of ageing people. New problems as acute as the old may well arise.

CHAPTER 4

Employment in Kirkby

In 1940 the Barlow Commission suggested that one of the disadvantages of suburban development in the inter-war years was the infrequent co-ordination of housing and industrial development, resulting in lengthy journeys to work and congestion in the centre of cities. It considered that the aim of a decentralized urban community should be 'to provide industrial and other occupational opportunities, preferably diversified, for a large, if not the greater proportion of the inhabitants'. This principle was emphatically endorsed by the New Towns Committee in 1946, who expanded the recommendation to 'all or a large proportion of the occupied population'. This was directly related to one of the earlier definitive characteristics of a New Town: its separation by at least ten to fifteen miles from any other urban centre so as to encourage the maximum possible independence, a requirement not always adhered to in recent years.[1] Since that time, with much practical experience of New Town development to be drawn upon, there has been some modification of this view of the independent New Town. In 1961, for instance, it was suggested by those concerned with the development of the proposed New Town at Hook that occupational balance should be thought the concern of the whole region and not just of the town itself.[2]

Kirkby's separation from Liverpool is minimal—a matter of some seven miles from the centre, only half a mile from the built-up area —and there is no doubt that this has tended to encourage continued dependence on the city as a source of employment for its wage-earners. The policy adopted by both Liverpool and Lancashire County Council[3] accepts this situation in the belief that Kirkby should be considered a part of the greater Merseyside area, and that not only will many Kirkby residents work outside the estate but that industrial development within it should be for the benefit not only of Kirkby but also of other Merseyside workers. At the initial planning stage officials did not in any case believe it practical to provide the distribution of jobs in the town which would be required

1. For example, East Kilbride is less than five miles from Glasgow.
2. *The Planning of a New Town*, L.C.C. 1961.
3. 1st Review, Kirkby Town Map, 1962.

for its total labour force. Such a policy, if followed, would also presuppose matching tenants to labour requirements: a proposal made in fact in 1955 by Lancashire County Council[4] but considered impractical in view of Liverpool's urgent need to find housing for so many living in overcrowded conditions.

In 1947, when development of the Kirkby Trading Estate began round the nucleus of the Royal Ordnance Factory, 5,000 people were employed on the estate. Industrial development was at that time encouraged by Liverpool Corporation's power under the Liverpool Corporation Act (1936) to sell leases at minimal rentals and allow long-term repayment for accommodation. When Merseyside was designated a Development Area in 1949, the Board of Trade was able to make additional contribution by its powers to allocate Industrial Development Certificates and building licences. In this respect Kirkby was given favoured treatment and the growth of industry proceeded rapidly, so that by 1959, when the greater part of residential development was complete, it was estimated that between 15,000 and 16,000 were employed on the estate.[5] In 1961 employment had increased to 18,000 while the total number of Kirkby residents employed in any area or unemployed was nearly 19,000.[6] It was considered at this time that there was a 'rough balance of jobs available and persons wanting jobs'.[7] The 1961 Sample Census shows that of these 19,000 a little over 9,500, or about half, were working outside the Urban District, the great majority in Liverpool (Table 36, Appendix A). A slightly higher proportion of men than women made up this group.

In 1961 over 13,000 people were coming to work in Kirkby from outside, again mainly from Liverpool. This means that in all over 16,000 men and nearly 7,000 women were involved in entering or leaving Kirkby in the journey to work.[8] The proportion of employed Kirkby residents working outside the Urban District is very much higher than is usual in New Towns. In Crawley, for instance, the figure is as low as 5 per cent, though where the co-ordination of industry and tenancy is less rigorous, 30 per cent is a more usual figure. By 1966 the balance had become rather more favourable for the residents. The total number of jobs available in Kirkby was then 27,500 and the number of residents in or out of employment was

4. Lancashire County Council Officers Overspill Development Services Sub-Committee, 1955.
5. A detailed account of the Kirkby Industrial Estate is given by H. Gentleman, 'Kirkby Industrial Estate: theory versus practice', in *Merseyside Social and Economic Studies*, ed. R. Lawton and C. Cunningham, Longman, 1970.
6. 1961 Sample Census.   7. 1st Review, Kirkby Town Map, 1962.
8. Corresponding figures for 1966 were 15,500 working in Kirkby though resident outside, nearly 19,000 men and just over 7,000 women entering or leaving Kirkby to work.

24,300. Less than half by this time were going outside Kirkby to work, though taking men alone the proportion was just over half; only a third of employed women worked outside Kirkby.

If Kirkby is to be considered in relation to the provision of employment for Merseyside workers as a whole, it faces a serious difficulty in that a large proportion of unemployed in the area, and especially long-term unemployed, are unskilled workers, often unused to the discipline of factory life. The majority of openings on the estate, as in most trading estates, have been from the first for workers with some training, semi-skilled by Ministry of Labour standards, and the proportion required has continually increased. In the early years development was hindered by a lack of suitably trained semi-skilled and skilled workers. Preliminary training was given extensively, although this led to a very high labour turnover. Even now relatively high absenteeism and poor management–worker relations in a number of Kirkby factories is related by some to the fact that many workers are conditioned to casual labour and so are less troubled than is usual by the possibility of dismissal.

In spite of the intention not to allocate Kirkby houses on the basis of employment requirements, it was necessary up to 1954 to provide houses for over 10 per cent of key workers. These were mainly concerned with precision engineering, and many had come from a considerable distance. By 1965, when there was an estimated 22,000 to 24,000 jobs in Kirkby, little training was given by the firms themselves, and most of the skilled labour and much semi-skilled labour came from outside the estate, particularly from north Liverpool, though generally workers were and still are drawn in from a 25-mile radius. Unskilled labour alone is largely provided by Kirkby itself.

Kirkby's great contribution to the Merseyside employment problem has been to continue the much-needed industrial diversification and expansion begun in the two other major industrial estates at Aintree and Speke. The influence of these three projects, together with the advent of Ford's factory at Halewood, have radically changed the character of an area which before the war was tied to a few vulnerable and declining industries. They have undoubtedly played a significant part in the definite though slow improvement in the employment situation.

Unemployment in Merseyside is now largely confined to the unskilled, the group who are the least affected by the new situation.[9] However, a comparison of manual grades between 1951 and 1961

9. See E. Gittus, 'A study of the unemployed of Merseyside', chapter 11 in *Merseyside Social and Economic Studies*, ed. Lawton and Cunningham, for a detailed analysis of this problem.

from Census data does indicate an upward shift in over-all levels of skill in the Liverpool area resulting from an increase in the proportion of semi-skilled and a decrease in unskilled workers (Table 6). The latter may be exaggerated to some extent as a result of the under-representation of large households in the 1961 Sample Census but it should not be entirely discounted.

TABLE 6

Grades of manual workers in the Liverpool area

Grade	1951	1961
	%	%
Skilled	51	50
Semi-skilled	16	26
Unskilled	33	24

1966 Census figures correspond closely to those of 1961.

The emphasis on manufacturing industry in the estate is shown by a comparison of the proportions employed in each of the main groups of industry in Liverpool and Kirkby (Table 7). While the

TABLE 7

Employment in Kirkby and Liverpool by groups of industry, 1961

	Kirkby estate			Liverpool C.B.		
Industry	Males	Females	All	Males	Females	All
	%	%	%	%	%	%
Agriculture and mining	1	—	1	—	—	—
Production	40	21	61	31	14	45
Services	24	13	37	32	23	55
Defence	1	—	1	—	—	—
Total	66	34	100	63	37	100

ratio of male to female workers is approximately 2 : 1 in both areas, the distribution between production and service industries differs considerably. The proportion 60 per cent manufacturing to 40 per cent service industry is one generally found in New Towns.

Kirkby has a great advantage over many estates and New Towns in requiring a relatively high proportion of female workers. About

40 per cent of those employed are women, with few exceptions semi-skilled or unskilled, working in clothing manufacture or processing, many coming from outside Kirkby. The 1961 Sample Census shows that 32 per cent of all married women in Kirkby had some kind of employment and 13 per cent worked part-time. By 1966 the proportion working had risen to 55 per cent though the proportion of these in part-time and full-time employment remained much the same. From the Kirkby survey it would appear that the proportion of women with children, living with their husbands, who were in employment was rather smaller than for women generally, only 10 per cent working full-time and 15 per cent part-time.

In a survey of the Crown Street area of Liverpool made in 1962 and 1963 very similar figures were obtained.[1] In the summer of 1962, 31 per cent of married women with children worked, 14 per cent full-time and 17 per cent part-time. Slightly fewer worked in the following winter, possibly a seasonal fluctuation (Table 8). It would seem

TABLE 8

*Employment of married women with children in Kirkby,
1960 and the Crown Street area, 1962–3*

Area	Not working		Working full-time		Working part-time		Total	
	No.	%	No.	%	No.	%	No.	%
Kirkby, 1960	180	75	25	10	37	15	242	100
Crown Street*								
Summer 1962	89	69	18	14	22	17	129	100
January–March 1963	84	74	12	11	17	15	113	100

* Source: E. Gittus, unpublished data.

probable from these figures that both in Liverpool and in Kirkby, given available local employment, those able and wishing to work did so; and that living away from relations, who were likely to be at hand in Liverpool to mind the children, did not in fact affect the position.

In Kirkby at the time of the survey about 40 per cent of the households contained more than one wage-earner; in about 16 per cent of cases these were children over school-leaving age. This contrasts strongly with the 1956 Crown Street households where 41 per cent contained more than two wage-earners and a quarter of the wage-earners in the area were women working full-time. It may be

1. E. Gittus, unpublished data.

assumed that as the Kirkby population ages there will be a tendency towards this more typical Merseyside pattern.

The occupations of all members of households in the survey in employment were recorded and classified according to the Registrar-General's socio-economic classification (Table 37, Appendix A). In the following sections of this report reference is generally made only to the occupation of the head of household. There were no significant differences between the distribution of social class groups of heads of household in the two samples. In Table 9 this is compared with the distribution found in Crown Street in 1956 and at the 1961 Census in Kirkby and Liverpool.

The proportion in social classes I and II in Kirkby is very low: most professional and managerial workers on the estate live on the coast or in more rural areas of the north. Non-manual groups generally are of much smaller size than in Liverpool, and even the 1956 Crown Street area. This is largely due to the lack of corner shops, small businesses, pubs, and hotels in Kirkby; in most parts of the Crown Street area shopkeepers and small employers formed the majority of those in non-manual grades, and a high proportion of the remainder were in personal service.

Well over four-fifths of heads of household in both samples were manual workers and over half of these were semi-skilled or unskilled. This compares with a proportion nearer to two-thirds in Liverpool, distributed about equally between skilled and semi- or unskilled. Kirkby, like many other large-scale housing estates, has been described as a one-class town; from these figures the description would appear to be justified. It should, however, be added that the non-manual element is somewhat understated in the survey sample, in which the (then) small areas of private building were excluded, but the 1961 Census figures indicate that this made little difference to the proportions.

It is interesting that although the proportion of non-manual workers living in Kirkby in 1966[2] had not changed from 1961 there was by 1966 a rather higher proportion of resident skilled and semi-skilled male workers and a lower proportion of unskilled (Table 9). This may be one result of Kirkby's programme of private house construction which would be most likely to attract workers in these groups who are increasingly ready to buy modern houses of a reasonable price; or it may be the result of selective migration—a possibility which will be discussed in Chapter 5. Private houses were built in the town between 1961 and 1966 and these are attractive and low-priced, their appearance contrasting sharply with the rest of the estate. Although it does not appear, as was at one time hoped, that

2. 1966 Sample Census.

they have brought in any significant numbers of professional or managerial workers, a second result of the construction of these houses may well have been to release some of the rented houses to younger tenants. Nine per cent of Kirkby residents moved to another part of the town between 1961 and 1966,[3] and it is probable that this included some making a change of tenure.

Nearly 5 per cent of the General and 15 per cent of the Crown Street sample were unemployed at the time of the survey. Of the 7 out of 12 unemployed with known occupations in the General sample, 6 were unskilled or semi-skilled manual workers and only one, a ship's repairer, was skilled. Three of the remaining 5 were disabled. Eight of 15 unemployed men in the Crown Street sample were unskilled or semi-skilled and 5 were skilled. However of these five, three were unemployed because of illness and one was learning a new trade at a government training centre. The usual occupations of the remaining two are not known.

The social class distribution of a sample of the 1958 intake population given in Table 9 is very similar to the over-all distribution at the time of the survey. This confirms the survey finding that although about two-thirds of the household heads in each sample changed either their job or their firm after removal to Kirkby, over half of these had remained in the same socio-economic group. About one-sixth in both samples who had changed their jobs had improved their position, half of these moving from unskilled to semi-skilled occupations. None in the Crown Street sample had worsened their position, while nearly a quarter of those in this sample whose circumstances were changed had previously been unemployed. On the other hand, only one respondent in the General sample had previously been unemployed, while nearly a quarter had moved either from skilled to semi-skilled, semi-skilled to un-skilled, or, in three cases, from shop-keeping to skilled manual work (Table 38, Appendix A).

It is very probable that in many cases a move to less skilled work was considered worthwhile if the cost of the journey to work was thereby reduced. This occurred in Macclesfield where 7 per cent of those moving from Manchester changed to a local job of lower status and wage in order to save travelling costs on the eighteen miles' journey. An additional 12 per cent obtained local work in the same occupation as before, but with a lower wage.[4] Similarly in Winsford, nearly half those men changing their job after moving from Man-chester lost in status and wages.[5] High travelling costs were a

3. Ibid.
4. J. N. Jackson, 'Dispersal—success or failure', *Journal of the Town Planning Institute*, xlv (1959).
5. H. B. Rodgers and D. T. Herbert, *Overspill in Winsford*, Keele, 1965.

TABLE 9

*Social class distribution of Kirkby survey employed
heads of household, and males employed in Kirkby,
the Crown Street area, and Liverpool C.B.*

Social class*	General sample	Crown St. sample	1958 intake sample	1961 Census	1966 Census	Crown St. 1956	L'pool 1961 Census
		Kirkby estate					
		Heads of household			All occupied males		Heads of house-hold	All occu-pied males
	%	%	%	%	%	%	%
Non-manual:							
I and II	2	4	2	4	4	14	10
III	10	11	11	10	10	15	16
Total	12	15	13	14	14	29	26
Manual:							
III	40	41	39	39	41	29	37
IV	20	16	24	24	25	21	19
V	28	28	24	23	20	21	18
Total	88	85	87	86	86	71	74
Total all groups	100	100	100	100	100	100	100
Not occupied (% of all heads)	11	29	11	N.K.	N.K.	24	N.K.

* Registrar-General's Classification of occupations: see Table 37, Appendix A.

significant cause of dissatisfaction with Kirkby. Two-thirds of the
General and three-quarters of the Crown Street householders were
paying over 7s. 6d. a week for their daily journey to work by public
transport, probably for most a considerable increase over their
costs when living in the city (Table 39, Appendix A). Over half in
both samples were using public transport, while only one-fifth were
able to walk or cycle to work (Table 40, Appendix A). Less than
one-fifth used a private car, motor-cycle, or moped at the time of
the survey. Kirkby differs in this respect from the characteristic
southern New Town in which cycles and cars are much used for the
journey to work: 58 per cent in Harlow New Town used cycle or
car in 1961, compared with 14 per cent in Kirkby. A rapid increase

in car ownership may be expected, however, and with it a demand for garage accommodation, which is at present rarely available. The 1966 Census gives some information on this point, though relating to all employed persons rather than heads of households. At this time a very similar proportion to that in 1960 was still using public transport to get to work and 13 per cent were using a car (Table 40, Appendix A). By then one-quarter of the households had cars though only a half of these were able to garage them, the remainder leaving them outside.

This dependence on public transport is closely related to the substantial employment of Kirkby residents well outside its boundaries: this applied at the time of the survey to over two-thirds of the General and about four-fifths of the Crown Street heads, a figure slightly higher than that given by the 1961 Census. Table 10 gives the

TABLE 10

Place of employment of Kirkby heads of household

Place of employment	Kirkby survey				1954 residents*	
	General sample		Crown St. sample			
	On arrival	At survey	On arrival	At survey		
	No. %	No. %	No. %	No. %	No. %	
Kirkby	19 10	54 30	2 2	23 21	245 20	
Liverpool	86 47	72 39	50 46	41 38	561 46	
Lancashire (excluding Kirkby and Liverpool)	29 16	17 9	6 6	6 6	16 1	
Cheshire	11 } 9	7 } 7	8 7	2 } 5	43 4	
Elsewhere	1	1	9 8	2	168 14	
Not fixed, not known, etc.	37 18	32 15	33 31	34 30	182 15	
Total	183 100	183 100	108 100	108 100	1,215 100	

* Source: Lancashire County Council Planning Department.

place of employment of the head of household in the two samples at the time of the survey, and at the time of transfer to Kirkby, and compares this with a sample of Kirkby householders in 1954. Significantly more in the General sample than the Crown Street sample worked in Kirkby at the time of their move, and in the General sample itself significantly more of the pre-1956 residents had done so. It is possible that a number of these were concerned with the early development of the estate and were therefore more likely to opt for Kirkby when stating a preference for the locality of their new residence.

In both samples, however, there has been a marked change in the location of employment between the time of the move into Kirkby and after residence for a number of years. It appears that this change to Kirkby employment had increased with time in the past and may, therefore, be expected to grow in the future as further opportunities arise within the estate. The change has been almost entirely at the expense of Liverpool. It is significant in this respect that an estimated 45% of Kirkby juveniles now work on the estate, and this again is a proportion which will undoubtedly increase. A comparison of 1961 with 1966 Census data confirms this (Table 36, Appendix A), though women appear to have taken more advantage of local employment in the meantime than men. However the trend away from Liverpool has continued, although to some extent there has been a diversion to other trading estates outside the city. Whiston, where the Ford works are situated, has been particularly successful in attracting workers from Kirkby.

In spite of the improvement that may be expected in the future, a high proportion of the present Kirkby residents will for many years be making a long and costly journey to work. A comparable situation in estates at Worsley, Langley, and Bristol has been, as at Kirkby, a major cause for dissatisfaction. Wilmott reports that in similar circumstances in Dagenham between 1931 and 1958 there has been a shift in the socio-economic structure of the estate, which has eventually become modified, from one very similar to the Kirkby pattern to one which corresponds more closely with national proportions;[6] occupational changes between 1961 and 1966 in Kirkby suggest that this has begun here. This has led in Dagenham to a significant increase in local employment, but undoubtedly the increase has been attained at the cost of initially high residential mobility with its accompanying social disturbance, a crude method of adjustment.

Hilda Jennings sees the importance of reducing the journey to work not only in economic terms but also because excessive time spent in travel reduces the amount left for social activities and leisure interests;[7] she considers this important enough to suggest that the conjunction of workers and workplace as a matter of simple proximity of workers to industry is not sufficient in itself and that a balance of more than numbers is required. The scale of the problem would

6. P. Willmott, *The Evolution of a Community*, Routledge and Kegan Paul, 1963.
7. H. Jennings, *Societies in the Making*, Routledge and Kegan Paul, 1962.

have been considerably reduced if some matching of tenants to jobs had been possible. This is a particularly difficult course in estates developed mainly to house an overspill population, although it has occurred at Winsford where most of the local employment is for unskilled workers and the selection of Manchester tenants has been related to suitable vacancies. Such a policy is also followed in the New Merseyside Towns at Skelmersdale and Runcorn where houses are directly allocated to firms for their employees.

The majority of Kirkby tenants, however, have moved out of central areas of the city where for economic reasons a high proportion of unskilled workers have settled. It is possible that a greater number of openings could be provided for them by inducement to suitable firms, but the present trend is towards industry largely employing labour with some degree of skill. R. Nicholas, who was responsible for the Manchester Plan, considers that the likelihood of large-scale complementary residential and industrial development in new development areas is too fanciful for serious consideration, and comprehensive overspilling should, therefore, be designed so that travel to and from the old places of work may be carried on for some years at least.[8]

Some advance to a less one-sided population appears to have been made since 1961 by the provision of private houses. Skilled workers now often have the means and prefer to buy a house of their own choice rather than rent, and it has already been suggested that the slight increase in the proportion of skilled workers by 1966 may have been in part a result of building private houses which may have attracted some who would otherwise have lived away from the estate.

A positive approach to the development of skill would be to provide comprehensive training schemes for adults. At present the younger Kirkby residents are relatively well catered for: the comprehensive schools and Technical College provide technical courses which are closely co-ordinated with the requirements of local industry; group apprenticeship schemes have been started by the smaller firms and about 30 per cent of Kirkby juveniles are in apprenticeships of some kind. This will lead to some increase in locally available skill in the future. At the present time, however, training for adults appears to be negligible. This is a complex problem requiring co-operation at all levels, but it might be considered in any study concerned with the location of industry.

8. Quoted by L. E. White in *New Towns*, National Council for Social Service, 1951.

CHAPTER 5

Stability and change

When a considerable number of people express the wish to break away from an environment which has been a source of companionship and protection through family and social contacts, this may be seen as an indication of a change in values of more than local significance. Klein has pointed out that housing estates are not the only places where change occurs but that 'the break with tradition which a geographical move entails allows other social forces to make a relatively more forcible impact'.[1] The implication is that social forces leading to change are independent of a particular location; it is the speed at which changes take place which may be influenced by circumstances such as the move to a housing estate.

Certainly in Crown Street in 1954 there were plenty of indications of impending change—underlying currents of dissatisfaction beneath the apparently stable surface, new uses for old property and new tenants with new values. Perhaps the strongest impression of the area which is left by the report is one of heterogeneity, and yet within each of the eight sectors found by the authors to vary significantly in character, there is the same indication that this is an area in transition and that, like it or not, the observed scene is unlikely to persist. The great majority of Crown Street residents had lived in the locality for at least ten years and more than half were born within the ten central city wards and the dockside area. In Low Hill and Smithdown wards a particularly strong attachment to the area was evidenced by length of stay, for nearly three-quarters of husbands or wives were born locally. Many had started their married life in their parents' houses and on moving out had not gone far, the tendency still surviving for parents to bespeak houses from their landlords for their children or to pass on the tenancy of their own houses. To the superficial observer, perhaps, this area is a Liverpool 'Bethnal Green', the link between mother and daughter an evident one, the extended family a social reality. Yet even here, although not yet translated into any large-scale action, dissatisfaction with the environment was sufficient to induce in nearly half of those living in these conditions (43 per cent in Low Hill and 44 per cent in Smithdown) an expressed wish to move away. The most significant

1. *Samples from English Cultures*, vol. 1, p. 220.

and strongest evidence of changing values was the increase in this proportion to more than half where resident heads of household were below the age of 50 years. Similar tendencies, though for slightly lower proportions of residents, were discovered in other parts of the Crown Street area and have been found in other urban situations such as in Swindon[2] and Barton Hill.[3]

The reasons given by the younger Crown Street couples for their wish to leave were largely associated with the need for a better house and a more advantageous environment, physically and educationally, for their children; a reflection, it would seem of a belief in their right to share at least some of the advantages until very recently only available to any degree to the middle and upper classes of society. This was confirmed by the fact that over half of those wanting to move (57 per cent) would prefer the outer residential areas—the areas where the new housing estates are situated, with their up-to-date amenities. With this in mind, therefore, it is interesting to observe the position from the other side. The wish for environmental change was undoubtedly present in Crown Street, and it may be inferred that it was becoming more widespread. How far was this wish fulfilled by the move to Kirkby?

Corporation housing estates acquire reputations which in general appear to be related closely to length of construction and the type of adjacent private housing. Norris Green, Liverpool's first large housing estate, was seen in 1929 as a low-status area because a higher proportion of its houses than in other corporation property were of the 'non-parlour' type. By the 1950s, when many of its houses contained residents of pensionable age, its child population had diminished from 34 per cent to 23 per cent[4] and its houses appeared substantial in comparison with those more recently built; it had become one of the more sought-after estates. Other long-standing estates also within a generally middle-class area, such as those at Childwall and Knowsley, similarly recovered from an earlier reputation for 'low class' tenants and are similarly well considered. Kirkby satisfied neither criterion. Isolated from the city in ghetto-like seclusion, the young resident families soon settled into a child-dominated society. Gangs of uncontrollable youngsters brought notoriety to the town and Kirkby became known throughout Merseyside as a vandal's paradise and a criminologist's challenge. It is very possible that the simple concentration of children at their most socially

2. J. B. Cullingworth, 'Swindon social survey', *Sociological Review*, ix (1961).
3. Jennings, *Societies in the Making*.
4. Estimates based on figures given by N. Williams, *Problems of Population and Education in the New Housing Estates*, Liverpool Ph.D. thesis, 1938, and Department of Social Science, 'A Norris Green Study', *Journal of the British Association of Social Workers* (July 1971).

destructive stage into a relatively small area in place of dispersal throughout inner Liverpool gave the illusion of a total youth population of delinquents. Surprisingly, no separate figures for juvenile delinquency are available for Kirkby so no exact comparison can be made. It might be added that many Kirkby residents and even some Kirkby children[5] resented the reputation they had acquired and considered it unfair saying it was 'not as bad as you read about' and 'I laugh at people who pull Kirkby down and make it worse than it really is'.

Nevertheless, the damage to Kirkby's reputation on Merseyside was immense and would certainly affect how many people made it one of their three choices of estates to the Housing Department when applying for a tenancy. It is perhaps not surprising that 29 per cent of Crown Street families specifically said that they had not wanted to move there. Rather more families in the General sample said this—36 per cent in all, still a minority but a sizable one. In fact about the same proportion in each group had also made Kirkby their first choice, the remainder being those without any preference in either direction; and it might be said that about two-thirds of Kirkby's residents had not initially been distressed by their being allocated a dwelling in the town. The difference in the proportion of Crown Street and General households with no wish to move to Kirkby was a significant one; so too was the difference in the proportion of those willing to move to any locality, out of the centre or not, illustrating the degree of dissatisfaction felt by young Crown Street families for their living conditions evident in the earlier survey (Table 11). Some evidence that the proportion of declared unwilling

TABLE 11

Wish to move to Kirkby originally

	General sample n = 183 %	Crown St. sample n = 108 %
No wish to move to Kirkby	36	29
Accepting move to Kirkby:		
Kirkby first preference or no dislike of Kirkby	38⎫	22⎫
Wish to move anywhere out of the centre of Liverpool	4⎬59	13⎬68
Wish to move anywhere at all	17⎭	33⎭
Other or no information	4	3

5. Mays, *et al.*, *School of Tomorrow*, chapter 6.

Kirkby immigrants had been inflated as a result of later difficulties is suggested by the tendency for relatively more of those paying rather higher than average rents to be among them, though it might be that those paying unsubsidized rents would be the better off and therefore more likely to see residence in Kirkby as a social decline.

When respondents were asked what aspects of Kirkby were considered preferable to their previous place of residence, half the responses were related to the cleaner and healthier environment. Typical comments were:

We've never needed a doctor since being here.

It's a much healthier place, my son's bad chest has been better since coming.

The children like it better than the town—I wouldn't go back if I had the rent for nothing.

The only other factors mentioned by any number were spaciousness and the quality of the housing (Table 41, Appendix A). On the debit side, Kirkby failed in more social requirements such as neighbourliness and convenience for shops, entertainments, or seeing relatives (Table 42, Appendix A). Significantly more former Crown Street residents found people less neighbourly in Kirkby, but separation from relatives did not seem to be of as great importance for either group, probably because whereas relatives were still in contact, a friendly relationship with neighbours needed to be built up anew.

It would therefore seem that about one-third of the Kirkby residents had been moved into the town against their will. The same proportion, although not entirely the same people, disliked the town sufficiently to wish to move away (Table 12). Ten per cent of those initially unwilling to come (so they said) had become reconciled. Rather less than half the households in both samples had become, at the least, used to Kirkby and said that if given a choice they would remain. This group, together with those unprepared to state any preference, amounted to two-thirds of both samples. The great majority of those in the General sample who wished to move away apparently would not choose to return to their previous homes and it seemed not to be the loss of city life that disturbed most of them so much as a general dislike of the area. On the other hand, about one-third of the previous Crown Street residents who wanted to go did say they wanted to go back to the city centre, and about the same proportion to some other part of Liverpool which was not a housing estate (Table 12). The greater strength of ties with the city shown by these residents is understandable considering the length of time so many had lived there.

TABLE 12

Wish to move away from Kirkby or to remain

	General sample n = 183	Crown St. sample n = 108
	%	%
Wish to move away from Kirkby:		
To centre of Liverpool	4	12
To some other local authority estate	4	6
To other part of Liverpool, not local authority estate	2	10
To any other accommodation which was not local authority	1	2
To any other destination	21	3
No location specified	2	2
Total wishing to move away	33	34
Wish to remain in Kirkby subject to:		
Change of residence	19	15
Change of locality	2	6
Other condition	1	0
No specified condition or no answer	23	26
Total willing to remain	44	47
Don't mind, don't know, and no answer	23	19
Total all groups	100	100

A more detailed analysis of those wishing to leave disclosed some interesting associations. Some factors which might be expected to be of significance such as rent paid, location of employment, or the basis of rehousing (redevelopment as opposed to those applying through the housing department) were not in fact of importance, and neither was the type of household or neighbourhood lived in. There was, however, a tendency for more of the recent than the old-established tenants to wish to leave; so did significantly more of those paying 7s. 6d. or more a week for their journey to work and, in the General sample, those living in high block flats.

Factors which appeared to be of most importance were those associated with social contacts. For example, those who preferred their previous neighbours to their present ones were more likely to wish to move but those who said they got on well with their present neighbours were less likely to do so. In the Crown Street sample, those respondents seeing their relatives less often than they did before coming to Kirkby and not making many contacts locally were more likely to want to leave, and there was a tendency towards this attitude also among those from both groups who kept in touch with friends and neighbours from their old homes and who went to entertainments wholly outside Kirkby.

The earlier Crown Street survey shows that many in Kirkby had left a situation where the extended families kept in close touch and these people had therefore experienced a sudden and considerable reduction in their contacts outside the home. However unsatisfactory life had been in physical terms, these ties, probably accepted as part of the day-to-day experience, must have gone some way to compensate for the difficulties of living in a decaying and deteriorating environment. Although they wanted to move, the reality of the break away would inevitably bring problems which might lead some of them to feel at least temporarily that they had lost more than they had gained. One such housewife said: 'If I'd known it would be like this, I'd have waited—you don't realize you've gone from bad to worse.'

Loss of contacts hitherto taken for granted must have been accentuated in Kirkby, as in most other new housing estates, by the lack of centres where new relationships could be built up in the early days—shops for the women and pubs for the men. Even when these were provided—some years after the first residents had moved in— they were not the local centres such places are in the inner city. Young and Willmott,[6] among many others, mention the regret for the loss of corner shops by estate residents in their study of 'Greenleigh'.

The reaction of many of those ex-Crown Street residents, unhappy with Kirkby, may therefore be associated with their sudden enforced transition to a looser social and family network than they had previously experienced. They may be identified with Mogey's[7] 'status assenters'—those accepting the habits and standards usually seen as typical of working-class groups which include kin solidarity. Acceptance of change is difficult for them and is likely to be slow for they have been brought up in a long-standing situation to which they are expected to conform; yet the Crown Street survey showed that the desire for change was widely present. Among those with this desire it is probable that the new life will be accepted by the majority in time: the tendency is apparent in Kirkby when longer-term residents are compared with the more recent. Such a reorientation

6. M. Young and P. Willmott, *Family and Kinship in East London*, Routledge and Kegan Paul, 1957; Penguin, 1962.
7. *Family and Neighbourhood.*

must have occurred for the resident who said: 'Southdene was awful at first and now it is the nicest.' Willmott's study of Dagenham,[8] also a largely working-class estate, after a longer period of time appears to indicate that the process of accommodation is completed for many after early stress and that an essential component for its success is the development of a new kinship network as the next generation marries and settles down within the estate.

In Kirkby a number of more personal factors were also found to be associated with a dislike of the town, perhaps indicating 'status dissenters' who reject working-class norms and seek to achieve standards closer to those of the middle classes, becoming critical of those who accept a way of life which they have rejected. In Kirkby many of those who wish to leave the town say they are lonely, feel they have insufficient privacy, find that there are people in Kirkby they would prefer not to mix with, and feel that the town is not as 'good class' an area as some of the newer parts of Liverpool. Such are the people who said, for example:

There may be decent people here, but I haven't met them—the children are anything but trained.

I prefer not to mix with them [next-door neighbours]—they're interfering and noisy and won't let you be what you want to be.

It may be inferred that people feeling like this are less likely to settle down in Kirkby and will eventually, if circumstances permit, move away, perhaps buying a house in areas such as Maghull or Formby. For this group the change in values is complete, but their inability for the present to dissociate themselves physically as well as emotionally might be expected to lead to some difficulty and unhappiness.

Some evidence of the existence and relative proportions of these two groups is given in the Crown Street study when attitudes to education are examined. Status assenters typically wish their children as well as themselves to remain in their present social position and therefore rarely encourage them educationally. The study confirms that a low value was placed on education by most Crown Street families but that a 'quite small' group of parents wished to leave the district in order to obtain better schooling for their children, seeing this as a way of moving up the social ladder.[9]

These groups may be seen at either end of a process in which the old ways of working-class life associated with extreme poverty, an enforced lack of education and low aspiration inducing a need for mutual support will eventually disappear. Between the two extremes those who have moved from unmodified 'status assenting' may be recognized, content with an improvement in standards rather than

8. *The Evolution of a Community*, chapter 10.
9. Vereker, *et al.*, *Urban Redevelopment and Social Change*, p. 77.

a substitution of new ones. Among those are probably the proportion—about 20 per cent in both samples—who were ready to stay in Kirkby but subject to an improvement in accommodation. Although this was equally true of residents in each neighbourhood, significantly more from the Crown Street sample disliked the locality they were in and there was a tendency within this group, which contained a rather higher proportion of large families than the General sample, for those with three or more children under school-leaving age to want to move, no doubt to a larger house. In addition, significantly more of those living in flats wished to move. The unpopularity of this type of dwelling has already been discussed and there is no doubt that a combination of large young families often filling flats to the maximum and occasionally above it, the inadequency of sound-proofing and monotony of design are among factors leading to dissatisfaction, but the low status accorded to flat-dwellers may have been at least as important. Block flats seem to provide grounds for complaint both materially and socially: poor sound insulation and insufficient room on the one hand and the minimum opportunity for informal social contact on the other, as a result of being on a different level from the life of the street. In the survey of flat-dwellers made by the Ministry of Housing and Local Government[1] it was found that more than one-quarter of the Liverpool households interviewed had put in for a transfer, a large proportion simply wanting a different type of dwelling. One Kirkby flat-dweller said, 'All conversations can be overheard and even knocks on the door are confusing.'

Factors influencing those who wanted to change their accommodation within Kirkby again included some personal ones, confirming that their affiliations were at least in part with 'status assenters', for in both samples such people were more likely to say that they did not get on well with their neighbours and preferred the neighbours they had had at their previous home, which they considered a more friendly place than Kirkby. When respondents were asked to suggest particular aspects of their accommodation which they liked or disliked, most comments were general rather than specific (Tables 43 and 44, Appendix A). One feature frequently mentioned with appreciation was the bathroom, for many had moved from dwellings too old or too small to have one; this was a deficiency often mentioned in the Crown Street survey.

Generally it would appear that acceptance of Kirkby depended to a large extent on the social contacts made. Traditional working-class status assenters are likely to have most difficulty in achieving standards of contact comparable with those they have left behind,

1. *Families Living at High Density.*

and here the inclination will be to return to their old background depending on how closely they identify themselves with it. Status dissenters may well accept fewer contacts than before the move, but these must be of the right kind and so may be unattainable. Their inclination will be to move to an area of higher status. Those ready for change but limited in their objectives are likely to remain and form the nucleus of the future Kirkby, such as the two who said, 'People are more respectable here and try to make themselves a lot better', and 'I'm happier here—I speak to a lot of people.'

In any neighbourhood, whether privately or corporation-built, there will always be a proportion of residents who are dissatisfied with their surroundings and wish to move. The incidence of such a group might be expected to be at its highest in a new community where the bustle and noise of a busy city environment has been changed overnight to the quiet and unfamiliarity of an estate set in rural surroundings with few of the everyday amenities such as shops round the corner, frequent buses, and local jobs. The change is dramatic and can hardly be expected to occur without difficult adjustment—too difficult for many. The Kirkby survey suggests that moves away will be in different directions according to the self-ascribed status of the movers. Williams[2] describes emigrants from Norris Green as of two types: those who find the cost of the move too high because of increased rents and fares, and those who decide to find better accommodation or better opportunity by moving to the Midlands or south. In this estate, built between 1926 and 1929, 50 per cent of the original families left in the first eleven years and approximately 30 per cent within the first two years. At this time accommodation for vacating families was almost certainly more easily obtained than today, so that those seriously wishing to go were reasonably free to do so. Willmott's study of the Dagenham estate[3] after forty years and Williams's of Norris Green after twelve years both show that in time a shift in occupational and age structure occurs as those wholly unsuited move out leaving the more satisfied behind, including many children of the original tenants. This leads in time to a population which appears to have accepted the estate completely as their home.

Unfortunately no records were available of the number of Kirkby tenancies vacated each year, but the 1961 and 1966 Sample Censuses give a figure of 6 per cent moving out of Kirkby between 1960 and 1961 and 4 per cent between 1965 and 1966; the occupational shift[4] may also be relevant. Residents in corporation housing estates today

2. *Problems of Population and Education in the New Housing Estates.*
3. *The Evolution of a Community.*
4. See Chapter 4, p. 30.

are less free to move than owner-occupiers, depending upon exchanges (which are notoriously difficult to obtain from Kirkby) or success in finding more suitable accommodation for themselves—unlikely when these are the families who in most cases have been housed by the Corporation simply because they have been unable to house themselves. The movement out of corporation houses into private houses is growing and has been discussed in Chapter 4. However, this type of move is only feasible for the more prosperous; it may therefore be accepted that many more would leave if they could, although the 33 per cent of households apparently wishing to move away probably includes many who, although dissatisfied, would not in fact go if the opportunity arose. This proportion of would-be-leavers has been found on other estates. For example, nearly one-third of the housewives interviewed on a Sheffield estate in 1952[5] expressed a wish to leave and about the same proportion of Manchester families in Winsford in 1964[6] did so. On the other hand, in Worsley in 1960 only 17 per cent of rehoused families apparently wished to return to Salford.[7] The situation on this estate appears in many ways comparable to that in Kirkby, with a scarcity of local employment for the mainly unskilled male residents. Here the improved standard of housing seemed more appreciated than in Kirkby. The long and expensive journey back to work in Salford appeared to be the main cause of dissatisfaction with this estate, and to a lesser extent separation from relatives, but it was of interest that nearly all those expressing a wish to return qualified their statement by saying that they would want a house of the standard they had in Worsley. In addition very few indeed would return if this meant their living in a flat.

It is difficult to estimate whether dissatisfaction with the Kirkby estate could have been reduced by the development of more positive aspects of estate management including those concerned with social welfare and in particular the provision of facilities and amenities at the same time as the first full-scale arrival of families. A substitute for this low and painful evolution of a stable community should be attempted, although it is unlikely that a certain period of unrest at the initial stage could ever be eliminated. It should be recognized that Kirkby residents are not as homogeneous as they may appear and perhaps most efforts should be directed to the 'middle' group, ready to accept change but requiring help to meet it in the initial stages.

5. Liverpool Department of Social Science and Sheffield University, *Neighbourhood and Community*, Liverpool University Press, 1954.
6. Rodgers and Herbert, *Overspill in Winsford*.
7. J. B. Cullingworth, 'Social implications of overspill', *Sociological Review*, viii (1960).

CHAPTER 6

Family and neighbours

Opinions differ on the importance today of the extended family in a working-class area. In a relatively closed and static community such as that of Bethnal Green,[1] or Ship Street, Liverpool,[2] the evidence is strong and well documented that frequent meetings between women members of a family who live within easy walking distance leads to a dependence upon one another for social contact and mutual aid. There is also evidence that, probably as a result of greater ease of communication, close proximity to relations does not assume the same importance for younger married couples as it did for their parents. However much they may like to live near to their family, for many this is not a first priority. If a healthy environment and educational opportunity for their children are clearly obtainable only as a result of a move away, then the break is accepted, however regretfully.

In the 1956 Crown Street survey[3] it was found that there was a strong tendency for married children to set up home in the vicinity of their parents. For 40 per cent of the married heads there, the first home after marriage had been with one of the couple's (generally the wife's) parents. Nine per cent had their own children, now married, living with them at the time of the survey, and nearly one-quarter had married children living within a quarter of a mile's distance. All in all, a high proportion of the households in this survey had members of their family living close by or within easy travelling distance. Although it was suggested by the authors that this close association might contribute towards some people's reluctance to move from the district, it was pointed out that there was no clear relationship between the two and that almost the same proportion of those without their family living at hand showed the same reluctance. It has already been noted that the younger married heads were more ready to move from the district than others, nearly always for the benefit of their children whose well-being was clearly placed first.

The Kirkby survey appears to support the case that for most households the move away from relatives is not a major factor where

1. Young and Willmott, *Family and Kinship in East London.*
2. M. Kerr, *The People of Ship Street*, Routledge and Kegan Paul, 1958.
3. Vereker, *et al., Urban Redevelopment and Social Change.*

the popularity of the district is concerned. Few of the parents of Kirkby residents lived on the estate, and of the 7 per cent of all parents who did so, about one-quarter lived in the same house as their children. In the Crown Street district, on the other hand, 33 per cent of the heads and 53 per cent of their wives had parents living in the district at the time of the survey, figures which are comparable to the proportion of Crown Street sample married couples with parents living in inner Liverpool (Table 45, Appendix A).

There was little chance of parents moving to Kirkby, for the number of houses allocated to other than young couples with children is small. Brothers and sisters, on the other hand, were more likely to move to the estate, especially if they had been living nearby previously in an area scheduled for demolition or clearance. One respondent had a sister living in the same flat block with whom there was frequent contact. Another household was found to have three related households on the estate; in this case there was a family history of tuberculosis. About 13 per cent of heads or wives of both samples had brothers or sisters in Kirkby (Table 45, Appendix A).

There was even less opportunity for married children of Kirkby households than for parents to live on the estate, for until 1964, when Kirkby Urban District was able to begin a programme of house-building for their own residents, all houses were allocated to Liverpool families. Sharing was also discouraged strongly. Only twelve children of Kirkby families in the survey had formed separate households in Kirkby.

In spite of the separation entailed by the move out from Liverpool, however, contact was retained by visits in either direction. Kirkby is near enough to Liverpool for there to be relatively little difficulty in paying visits in either direction, but the short informal call which is usual where relatives live within a close area has inevitably been lost. Nevertheless, the great majority of parents and children of husbands or wives in both samples and well over half their siblings living in inner Liverpool saw their related families in Kirkby at least once a month (Table 46, Appendix A).

An example of the operation of this in practice is given in the Crown Street report:

The way in which family ties overcome geographical separation was well instanced in the case of Mrs. A. . . . Her daughter from Kirkby several miles away regularly visited her and in fact came daily to the Crown Street district to do her job as a children's nurse . . . Mrs. A. found relief from the deplorable physical conditions in which she was obliged to live by sandwiching regular visits to Kirkby between evenings at the pictures and attendance . . . at the parish church.[4]

4. Vereker, et al., Urban Redevelopment and Social Change, p. 69

A very slightly higher proportion of wives' relatives than husbands' were involved in the visiting. Only in the case of some relations of the General sample living in outer Liverpool or outside the city and the siblings or children of previous Crown Street residents living outside Liverpool were frequent visits (once a month or more) less usual. Although close proximity is clearly an important factor in maintaining a close relationship with relatives the proportion who are visited at some distance is a high one.

In the General sample most householders and their wives who saw their parents at least monthly did so both inside and outside Kirkby; the difference between the proportions who saw their parents only at Kirkby and only at the parental home outside Kirkby was small. There is no support for the supposition that visiting parents in Liverpool is more frequent than parents coming out to Kirkby to visit their children; visiting Kirkby is a normal occurrence for parents. It was unfortunate that the number of households with parents in Kirkby or children living away from home was too small for detailed analysis of any differences in the frequency of visiting parents or children nearby or in Liverpool. Most of the following discussion refers to siblings or to relatives in general for this reason.

It would seem to be inevitable that as time goes on less is seen of relatives living outside Kirkby. In the General sample significantly more of the households who moved in before 1956 than later arrivals considered that they saw less of their relatives than they did before moving, though this does not appear to apply to Crown Street households. The observation from the General sample is confirmed by the fact that significantly fewer of the heads of household who arrived before 1956 than those who arrived later see brothers or sisters living in inner Liverpool or outside Liverpool as often as once a month. The siblings of wives do not show this trend to such a marked degree but the tendency is there too.

There is no significant difference between the two samples in the proportion seeing their relatives at least once a month or less frequently, with the exception, already mentioned, of siblings of the head or wife living in outer Liverpool. The samples were also similar in their assessment of whether they now saw more or less of their relatives than before their move (Table 47, Appendix A). More than half in both samples said that they saw less of their relatives but on the other hand quite a sizable minority apparently saw more of them; this might be expected where a move to Kirkby by some other member of the family had occurred, but in the great majority of cases this was not so.

The admission of loneliness in Kirkby appears to be directly related to reduced contact with relatives after going to the estate.

'Loneliness' is a highly subjective term and generally researchers using it have accepted this limitation but still find it has value in its associations. Tunstall[5] has shown in his study of retirement pensioners that a higher proportion of those saying they were lonely were widows with children whom they saw infrequently. The association of loneliness in Kirkby with a lessened contact with relatives is comparable, and the important factor again appears to be the reduction of contact rather than a complete loss, for in Kirkby there did not appear to be any significant relationship with frequency as such, at least at the level of less or more than once a month. Those considering Kirkby to be a less friendly place than their previous residence were also more likely to be those seeing less of their relatives than previously. As a corollary to this, a significant number of families in the General sample seeing less of their relatives also considered that most of their friends lived in the original home area.

The interrelationship of contact with relations and friends has frequently been remarked: Young and Willmot, for example, emphasize that the family, 'far from . . . excluding ties to outsiders, acts as an important means of promoting them'.[6] Close contact with relations implies a widening circle of friends as introductions are made in pub, shop, or other meeting-place. Possibly the formation of friends through relatives as intermediaries is regarded as a sifting or protective mechanism without which there is uncertainty or suspicion preventing ready formation of contacts. This would explain why a large proportion in the General sample who do not see their relations as much as before moving are also those who find there are people in Kirkby with whom they prefer not to mix. In the same context, a large proportion of those who have little contact with their siblings in Kirkby have no contact at all with neighbours.

In stable areas of Crown Street such as Low Hill it seems likely that the conjugal relationship for many families was, at least until recently, traditionally working class in character—a segregated role relationship with close ties between mother and daughter on the one hand and on the other hand male association at the pub, club, and the football match. The frequency with which daughters set up home close to their parents was an indication of one side of this, but unfortunately no evidence was provided on the other, male aspect. Many community studies have shown changes in attitude leading to a greater participation by the younger husbands in domestic affairs and by their wives in social activities away from the home, changes which may largely be attributed to improved economic

5. J. Tunstall, *Old and Alone*, Routledge and Kegan Paul, 1966.
6. *Family and Kinship in East London*, p. 104.

circumstances and widened horizons. Again this is a change likely to be accelerated by the move to the suburban housing estate, enforcing as this does separation from the parents and a need to co-operate in setting up the new house, cultivating a garden perhaps for the first time and various do-it-yourself activities, particularly where money for new fittings is scarce.

Kirkby tenants on the whole give little impression of prosperity. No inquiry on income was made, for too much would have had to be taken into account—overtime, casual work, allowances, and so on. The very low car ownership is indicative, however, and it seems reasonable to assume that in a town with such a high proportion of semi-skilled and unskilled manual workers, many would find the move to a new house a financial burden. At the time of the survey it was noted that a substantial number of tenants had continued to use the furniture and other effects of their previous home: furnishings were often drab and well worn. For many households, therefore, if decorating was to be done it must be by the husband or wife. In fact all the Crown Street households except 16 (84 per cent) had done some decorating, even some who had been in occupation for less than a year. In more than one-third of those households both husband and wife were involved and the impression was given that redecorating was frequent. More than half the respondents thought that they spent more time on decorating in Kirkby than previously, though a third thought less (Table 48, Appendix A). A very variable amount of interest was taken in gardening but there were indications that this was growing. Gardens varied in size and those attached to the flats were too small and too over-run by children to provide much incentive. Nevertheless this, for many, new activity was again one likely to increase the time spent in the home.

In day-to-day family affairs therefore there is an indication of some change, but for most not a dramatic one. In general, close relatives are seen less often than before, but still frequently enough, while home-based activities have probably increased. The importance of continued contact with relatives is demonstrated, however, by the large number who rely on their family for help in times of illness. In both groups relatives living elsewhere are most likely to give help even when living some distance away. This was true of 41 per cent of households in both groups while the next most frequent arrangement was help from a relative living in the house: this was mentioned by about a quarter of the respondents. Unexpectedly, in the Crown Street survey the position indicated was the reverse of this, but this may have been because there the proportion of three-generation households was relatively high. Neighbours alone were not often mentioned by either group in Kirkby and only slightly more fre-

TABLE 13

Care in illness, Kirkby and the 1956 Crown Street area

Care by:	Kirkby survey				Crown St. 1956
	General sample		Crown St. sample		
	No.	%	No.	%	%
Relatives at home	45	24	33	30	44
Relatives elsewhere	76	41	44	41	22
Neighbours	12	7	4	4	12
Others or not known	25	14	14	13	} 22
Combination of above	25	14	13	12	
Total	183	100	108	100	100

quently in Crown Street, though a combination of neighbour and relative seemed fairly common in both locations (Table 13).

The absence of relatives was rarely commented on by respondents, in the way that the absence of acquaintances was mentioned, suggesting that the separation was not seen as of primary importance. Willmott and Young[7] report that in a private housing estate at Woodford where obviously choice of location has been exercised by the householders, those with working-class backgrounds tended to live nearer to their parents than those of middle-class origin, but the amount of contact was very similar in the two groups. Frequency of contact was certainly lower than that occurring in Bethnal Green but it was still high: for example, 63 per cent of Woodford residents had seen their mothers during the previous week compared with 74 per cent from Bethnal Green. On the other hand, Jackson[8] in 1959 found that nearly half the Manchester overspill families in Macclesfield whom he interviewed commented on their separation from relatives. In this community there was a great deal of dissatisfaction with school facilities and the availability of local employment. Jackson remarks that social discontent tends to be highest when allied to economic hardship, as was the case in this situation.

Cullingworth[9] in 1960 suggested that it was the older members of families in Worsley who particularly missed relatives, especially their children, and that for the younger couples financial factors and the journey to work were greater causes of dissatisfaction than loss of

7. P. Willmott and M. Young, *Family and Class in a London Suburb*, Routledge and Kegan Paul, 1960.
8. 'Dispersal—success or failure'.   9. 'Social implications of overspill'.

kinship ties. He also reported that in Swindon in 1961[1] those who found separation from relatives a hardship were usually those with parents who needed care, but that nevertheless only four wished to return to their former home for this reason. Cullingworth also comments that the weakening of kinship ties may even be welcomed where there has been a great deal of contact, as for example where the couple had previously 'lived in' with parents. One of the few Kirkby comments relating to separation was in answer to the question 'Do you feel lonely in Kirkby?'; the reply was 'No—Mother was awful—here I have someone to talk to.'

Cullingworth suggests that proximity rather than ties of kinship may lead to the frequency of contact which arises in overcrowded areas. A similar conclusion might well arise from Kirkby residents' responses on questions relating to this. There are strong indications that it is social contact itself which is missed, irrespective of whether this is contact with relatives or neighbours or casual acquaintances. Contact with relatives was retained, and though on a reduced level it appeared to be a satisfactory one. If contacts with non-relatives are adequate and of a satisfactory nature, then a reduction of those with relatives is not generally considered a cause for discontent. On the other hand it has already been seen that where Kirkby residents were asked in what way they preferred the place where they previously lived, greater neighbourliness there ranked high, particularly among those moving from Crown Street, and a poor relationship with present neighbours was associated with a wish to move. Proximity of relations appeared to be considerably less important, probably because good neighbours are lost and must be replaced while relations remain. The easy relationship with people seen day after day living in the same possibly difficult circumstances takes time to build up. On the new estate the process must begin afresh, complicated by unfamiliar surroundings. At the same time the break from an old to a new neighbourhood gives the opportunity for new standards to be set up, an opportunity which some will wish to take. The uncurtained window or the shabby furniture may be tolerated for the time being when the general dilapidation of the neighbourhood encourages little else, but where all are strangers such possessions take on a new importance as indicators of social attitudes and are used for assessment of social status. Klein[2] has described the development of new norms by such a 'social comparison process' using examples from Willmott's study of Dagenham. Kirkby follows the general pattern and shows again that many new estate residents under the acute social pressures which arise retreat into a desire for privacy. Time and again comments were made on

1. 'Swindon social survey'.   2. *Samples from English Cultures*, vol. 1.

these lines: 'I'm one who tries to keep to myself', 'I like to choose my own company', and 'When you don't bother them they say you are stuck up'; though in addition there were a few perhaps more perceptive and less ready to accept the barriers as impenetrable: 'Here they keep themselves to themselves, but are always ready to help', and 'People are more respectable here and try to make themselves a lot better.'

One great problem for the investigator who wishes to consider relationships between neighbours is, of course, to be sure that the term 'friend' or 'neighbour' is being interpreted in the same way by all respondents. In the Kirkby survey when frequency of contact was being investigated the words themselves were not used; instead respondents were asked whether and with what frequency they visited or were visited by anyone in their homes and whether they went out with anyone else shopping. The people concerned were then classified as up to three doors away and further. No significant differences in response to these questions arose between interviewers—which would have been likely if there had been differences of interpretation—and no differences arose according to whether the husband or wife was the respondent.

Another drawback is that the terms 'visiting' and 'going out with' generally denote activities of some formality, relating more closely to middle-class than working-class practices. In the minds of some respondents who did not claim either type of contact the terms may not have been seen as including visiting of what might be called the 'popping in and out' variety, or a highly informal visit to nearby shops. They would necessarily exclude chatting at front and back doors and on flat landings, which was observed frequently, and which indeed the interviewers had occasionally to interrupt. Informal interaction between residents is therefore understated, the more so as visiting less often than weekly, which was reported quite often, has been excluded. On the other hand, a substantial proportion of those households reporting absence of contact with any other household at Kirkby indicated quite firmly that they had nothing to do with neighbours at all.

Just over half the households in both samples said that they had contact with some other household which involved visiting or being visited more than once a week, while a quarter in the General sample and, rather less in the Crown Street sample (significantly so) said that they 'went out with' members of other households (Table 14). When people were asked how contact was originally made, the replies were mainly unspecific such as 'through being neighbours' and suggested that merely living nearby was the only factor involved (Table 15). Most acquaintances in Kirkby in fact lived 'within three

TABLE 14

Location of acquaintances visited and gone out with in Kirkby*

Location	Acquaintances visited		Acquaintances gone out with	
	General sample n = 183	Crown St. sample n = 108	General sample n = 183	Crown St. sample n = 108
	%	%	%	%
Next door and 2–3 doors away	39	37	19	12
In same road	16	17	5	3
Elsewhere in Kirkby	16	17	8	4
Those with acquaintances visited or gone out with	54	54	25	17
Acquaintances next door and 2–3 doors away *only*	24	27	—	—
In same street *only*	9	6	—	—
Elsewhere *only*	18	17	—	—

* Respondents may appear more than once in the upper part of this table.

TABLE 15

How acquaintances in Kirkby are made

How acquaintances are made	General sample		Crown St. sample	
	No.	%	No.	%
Through being neighbours	65	35	39	36
Through work	10	5	7	6
From previous residence	7	4	2	2
Other	22	12	18	17
No answer	1	1	2	2
Total with acquaintances	105	57	68	63
No acquaintances	78	43	40	37

doors away', and for about a quarter of both samples these were the respondents' only acquaintances. Other acquaintances were equally likely to live further away in the same road or elsewhere in Kirkby. Contacts in Kirkby would therefore appear to be on a very local basis and were far from evenly spread throughout the neighbourhood in which the household was living. Unfortunately there are no comparable data for Crown Street which could suggest what degree of isolation is indicated by nearly half the respondents in both groups admitting to no contacts in the way of visits to others.

It is of some interest that the proportion of households with some contacts of this type did not differ significantly between residents in houses and in block flats. One difference which did arise within the town was that there were significantly more households without such contacts in Northwood, the latest of the three neighbourhoods to be built. This difference did not appear to be related to length of residence, however, for no significant difference arose between households who had moved into Kirkby before and after 1956. Northwood's other characteristic is that it contains the highest proportion of children under five years old, and as such children tend to be at their most demanding at that age it may well be that the time available to their mothers for visiting and going out is considerably restricted.

It has been noted that an admission of loneliness appears to be associated with a reduced amount of contact with relatives, but it does not appear to be affected by the frequency of contact with neighbours for the number of such visits is not related. Here again Tunstall's[3] experience is relevant: his socially isolated people were not necessarily lonely, or vice versa. However, a significantly greater number of those who say they find Kirkby a less friendly place than their previous home have no local contacts.

In a survey of a Sheffield housing estate in 1952 it was suggested that attitudes to the neighbours frequently reflected attitudes to the estate.[4] In Kirkby only about a quarter of all respondents said that they found the town a less friendly place than their previous place of residence, though a rather higher proportion said that they had less to do with their neighbours than previously. On the other hand, only very few indeed in either sample would admit that they did not get on well with them (Table 49, Appendix A). This may reflect a detachment which is not unfriendly but will afford protection from a relationship which may not be compatible with the new social attitudes being worked out.

Significantly more of those who still visited friends in their previous home area said that they preferred their old neighbours, but this might be expected since a strong relationship would clearly be required to encourage continued visiting over this distance. These people were also more likely to say that they had less to do with Kirkby residents than with previous neighbours. An admission of

3. *Old and Alone.*
4. Liverpool Department of Social Science and Sheffield University, *Neighbourhood and Community*, Liverpool University Press, 1954.

loneliness is also strongly associated with a preference for former acquaintances, and combined with the greater likelihood they have of seeing less of their relatives than previously, it appears to be a reflection of a general 'homesickness' which favours the old home ground. These people who are lonely, prefer their previous neighbours and miss their relatives, are in the main the people who wish to move from either their present accommodation or from Kirkby itself, and who have already been identified as 'social assenters', disliking the enforced change and wishing to return to the comfort of a well-known physical and social environment.

Discontent with Kirkby to the point of wishing to leave has also been observed to occur among a greater proportion of residents in block flats than those in other accommodation.[5] It is not surprising to find, therefore, that significantly more of those living in block flats feel that they have less contact with neighbours than previously (though we have seen that there was no greater proportion of them without contact at all), and to find that those they know are less friendly. One flat-dweller, for example, said:

At Crown Street people stand at doors or sit on steps and talk across the street. At Kirkby they sit in their own back yard. If you come outside the door [in Crown Street] three or four people would stop and talk to you. You feel on your own up here—only going to shops gives you a break.

On the other hand, a significantly small proportion of those who have moved to Kirkby voluntarily by exchange or transfer find Kirkby unfriendly, and there is a tendency for those who previously lived in rooms to find the town at least as friendly as their previous home. A significantly greater proportion of such people said also that they now had more to do with their neighbours than before. Their previous experience may perhaps be compared with that of present Kirkby flat-dwellers. Living in close physical contact with others clearly does not automatically lead to friendly relationships and the stresses of semi-communal life may well in fact have an opposite effect.

An acceptance of Kirkby as a friendly place appears to be inversely related to affection for the earlier home and attachment to those who live there. About equal proportions of household members find Kirkby more friendly, less friendly, and much the same as their previous locality (Table 49, Appendix A). Significantly more of those with most friends in the area they left, however, say they have less contact with neighbours in Kirkby than previously, but this may well be a subjective judgement.

5. See Chapter 5.

The three groups with differing assessments of Kirkby's 'friend-liness', however, do not appear to be irreconcilable, for length of residence does appear to be associated to the extent that a significantly greater proportion of those who had lived in Kirkby at least four years at the time of the survey said that most of their friends were in the town. It has already been seen that time on this scale is not associated with the existence of contacts at the casual level, but it is possible that the term 'friend' has been taken in the later question to refer to a more developed relationship than did the earlier one.

Community studies in a number of localities indicate that status dissenters tend to find their desire to break away from what they see as a restricting background reinforced by the move to an estate. Here they may see an opportunity to achieve at least some of their ambitions: to provide themselves with some of the material comforts and their children with better educational opportunities. Klein[6] suggests that in doing so they become more than ever aware of the difference between themselves and those who cling to the old values and tend to resent their enforced close association with those they consider to be their social inferiors. For example, Kuper[7] found that the main barrier to a close association between neighbours on a Coventry housing estate were the status distinctions drawn between them on the grounds of 'respectability', though the criteria on which judgement of this quality was based varied between different groups of residents. Social position might be assessed on front room furnishings or the children's behaviour or cleanliness of the house, among other considerations. In Knowsley[8] many residents similarly distinguished between a 'better' part of the estate and the 'lower' end where many families from bombed areas had been housed, and where less acceptable standards of behaviour were believed to occur. Similarly in Sheffield[9] a distinction arose between the top and bottom ends of the estate based primarily on the slightly improved design of those later built houses at the bottom end.

In Kirkby an attitude of this type has already been seen to occur between neighbourhoods, Southdene being considered 'more select' and Westvale 'very rowdy'. For some residents the whole estate was socially undesirable. This was expressed by such comments as 'One is classed into a group only as fit for Kirkby', or 'There may be decent people here, but I haven't met them.' Others selected tenants of particular types of property for their distaste. For some unknown reason maisonette residents in Kirkby were considered particularly

6. *Samples from English Cultures*, vol. i.
7. L. Kuper (ed.), *Living in Towns*, Cresset Press, 1953.
8. *Neighbourhood and Community*.   9. Ibid.

undesirable by a number of respondents, provoking remarks such as:

I prefer not to mix with people in maisonettes. I don't like their habits though I like to be congenial to all regardless of class or colour.

Rough people seem to be in maisonettes—houses shouldn't be mixed with maisonettes.

The dissatisfaction of this group may well be accentuated by the town's reputation as an area where gangs flourish, vandalism goes unchecked, and the police are barely able to maintain the expected standards of social conformity—a reputation based on the earlier years of the estate, considered by many to be undeserved today. More comments were made on this aspect of estate life than on any other topic, usually in enlargement to the answers to two questions: 'Are there some kinds of people in Kirkby you prefer not to mix with? If yes, what sort of people?' and 'Do you think you have enough privacy?' Just over half the respondents in both samples said that there were people in Kirkby they preferred not to mix with, while one-third felt that they had not enough privacy. Neither appeared to be related to frequency of contact with neighbours, at least at the level considered, except that there was a tendency towards more of those who had some contact, both by visiting and being visited or by going out with neighbours, to say that they preferred not to mix with some people in Kirkby. When asked to say what sort of people these were, more than half made use of such terms as 'rough', 'common', 'dirty', 'of low morality', and so on. The remaining answers fell into a number of small categories, all of about equal size and which included teenagers, 'violent-types', 'la-di-da' people, Roman Catholics, and specific residents, with the exception of 18 per cent whose response (although they had agreed that there were people they preferred not to mix with) was that as they did not in fact mix with anyone, they could not say what kind of people these were. The respondents who answered 'No' to the question on mixing were mainly those people who find Kirkby a more friendly place than their previous home and say that they have more to do with their neighbours than before. A few comments show that some residents felt that they had done better socially by moving to Kirkby, for example: 'People are more respectable here—they try to make themselves a lot better', and 'People here are better than at [Crown Street]—they were a dirty lot in my house at [Crown Street].'

Many people, however, seemed to take the opposite view with remarks such as 'There are a better lot of people living in Scotland Road.'[1]

1. A formerly notorious downtown district of Liverpool.

The point of view of those who apparently mixed with no one was usually expressed in such a form as 'We keep to ourselves—live our own lives.' To these people the maintenance of their privacy must be essential, though it may be expected that the importance attached to privacy varies considerably from one person to another according to their personalities. However, it is clear from an analysis of answers to the question on privacy that the word had different interpretations. For example, there was a strong tendency for parents with children in the household under and over school age (but not of school age) to feel that they had insufficient privacy. Here obviously the area in which they lived can take little responsibility, though the type of accommodation may, and lack of privacy meant to them too much contact within the home. On the other hand there was a tendency for fewer of those residents over sixty years old, or of a younger age but on their own through widowhood or divorce, to say that they had insufficient privacy, and here the association seems to be with isolation. At the same time, a belief that their lack of privacy could be associated with Kirkby itself must have been held by many, for a large proportion who wished to leave the estate complained about it. These also again tended to be the people who found Kirkby a less friendly place than their previous residence and had less to do with their Kirkby neighbours than they had with their previous ones. Lack of privacy was to this unhappy group one more of many reasons for their discontent.

CHAPTER 7

Leisure activities

The Crown Street survey showed, to the evident surprise of the investigators, that the residents made little contact with social organizations. Only 9 per cent of the households contained children under fifteen years of age who belonged to a youth organization and only 2 per cent contained adolescents who were members, though provision for them was not in any case adequate in either number or hours available considering how many young people lived in the area. In nearly two-thirds of all households (62 per cent) no person of any age was attached to any social organization; but there was a positive association between length of residence and attendance, ranging from 48 per cent participation by those who had lived in the area for ten years or more to 28 per cent by those resident for less than five years.

Information on adult attendance at such organizations as co-operative guilds, mothers' unions, young wives' groups, working men's clubs, and political clubs was obtained, and it appeared that fewer of the retired than the occupied were involved and there was a slight tendency towards greater use by manual than non-manual workers. Church attendance was relatively high for a working-class district, perhaps because of the high proportion of Roman Catholics.

In Kirkby respondents were asked how often they had attended these organizations in the past and at present. For those aged twenty years and under, past attendance appeared to be of a similar order to that found in the earlier survey, and for adults rather lower. All age groups in both samples, however, showed significantly increased attendance in Kirkby, and taking households as a whole, nearly half had at least one member attending an organization, compared with about one-quarter before the move (Table 16). As might be expected under the circumstances, membership was predominantly of organizations inside Kirkby (Table 17). It also appears that newly arrived and older established residents equally took part. There was a tendency towards lower participation by those living in flat blocks, but the evidence was not conclusive.

This increased participation may well have been due to increased opportunity, for by the time the Kirkby survey was made there were a number of facilities available for young people and adults on the

TABLE 16

*Present and past attendance at meetings of organizations (by at
least one member of the household), Kirkby and the
1956 Crown Street area*

	Kirkby survey				
	General sample		Crown St. sample		Crown St.
Group attending	Past	Present	Past	Present	1956
	attendance		attendance		
All households with some members attending	%	%	%	%	%
	25	46	31	45	38
Member in age group:					
5–14 years	7	13	11	14	12
15–20 years	2	7	4	6	6
21 and over	18	36	19	33	24

TABLE 17

*Location of meetings of organizations attended at present
(by at least one member of the household)*

Location of meetings of organizations	General sample	Crown St. sample
	%	%
All outside Kirkby	5	6
Kirkby and outside	8	5
All inside Kirkby	42	42

estate. This, of course, was not true of earlier years, described by one
respondent as 'like Siberia'. It may also, at least in part, have been
further evidence of changing norms, though this is more difficult
to assess. Certainly by 1961 a good deal of effort had been made by
a number of voluntary bodies to provide recreational facilities, particularly for younger residents, partly in an effort to combat the well-
publicized delinquency in the town.

During the early years of the estate it was mainly the churches who
provided occasions for social activities, and the Roman Catholics
who were the most active, judging by the number of parish clubs set
up. These clubs are housed in church halls and are open most
evenings; they are licensed and run frequent bingo nights. The
Anglicans followed suit by setting up a youth club. Non-secular

organizations moved in at a later date while the non-conformists showed the least initiative in this respect.

It has already been mentioned that about half the Kirkby residents are Roman Catholic, but there is none of the physical segregation on the estate that is found in Liverpool where traditionally 'Orangemen' and Catholics form antagonistic groups in different residential areas, reaching a peak of mutual animosity on Orange Day. Tensions were occasionally evident in Kirkby, nevertheless, and the suggestion was made more than once that the Kirkby Catholics would eventually 'take over' to form a Catholic community. The segregation that occurs among the majority of schoolchildren may contribute to this lack of sympathy between denominations. Two of Kirkby's four comprehensive schools as well as two primary schools are Roman Catholic. While a small number of Roman Catholics may find their way to the secular schools, it is unlikely that the reverse situation would occur. Thus the children are generally separated in their school life and the adults in many of their leisure-time activities.

In 1961 there were five youth centres supported by the local authority. Two were held in small prefabricated buildings and three in secondary schools. Many young people at Kirkby belonged to one or more of these clubs at some time or other, and there was some movement of members from one club to another, each of which was said to have some distinct character of its own. The County Youth Officer, who gave much of his time to Kirkby, ran a training course for part-time paid youth centre wardens. The range of activities at the Westvale Youth Centre, which had its own building, was varied and the number of members impressive. It might therefore be said, contrary to generally held public opinion, that compared with other local authorities of its size the provision for youth in Kirkby was good, the more so since every church had either a youth group or made other provision for the needs of young people.

Nevertheless there is little doubt that when Kirkby's age structure is taken into account, there was a need for an increase in the provision of recreational facilities for young people and particularly for a higher standard of buildings and amenities. It is of interest that during the years following the survey facilities have been increased and further plans made, to the extent that it seems likely that Kirkby will become, if it is not already, one of the best provided towns of its size in the country.

The original Church of England youth club, Centre 63, is now grant-aided with a full-time leader, and is the largest of the Kirkby youth clubs with a membership of 650 and average nightly attendances of 150. In addition there are six maintained youth clubs with part-time leaders and four run by the churches on a voluntary basis, as well as organizations such as Scouts and Guides, Church Lads' Brigade, Air Training Corps, and so on. A sports stadium was built by the Urban District in 1964, incorporating a gymnasium, racing and cycle tracks, and an athletics arena. This is being expanded into a comprehensive sports centre which it is hoped will serve a much wider area than purely that of the town itself. Other youth centres are planned for the near future. Clubs are also run by the comprehensive schools for their own pupils.[1]

Yet in a survey made by the Divisional Education Officer for Kirkby in 1964, it was estimated that in spite of the considerable provision of facilities, three-quarters of the population between fourteen and twenty years old were still unattached to any organized youth group. It is, of course, quite possible that an expansion of services will not affect this group significantly as it may contain a large proportion of 'unclubables'. The fact that among both boys and girls in the survey 'staying in bed' was the answer most often given when they were asked to give an account of their usual way of spending Saturday and Sunday morning, and 'television' for Saturday evening and Sunday afternoon and evening, suggests that many have less of a regard for physical activity than might be considered suitable by their elders.

The attention paid to Kirkby's young people is largely a result of their reputation on Merseyside as a tough lot, given to associating in gangs, notorious for violence and anti-social activities such as wrecking telephone booths and smashing windows; though it has previously been pointed out that possibly the level of delinquency characteristic of central areas of all large cities becomes highlighted when concentrated in a relatively smaller area. Other theories have been provided by various authorities, however, including a reduction of parental control (though this is probably in any case looser among the working class than middle class) as a result of the dis-organization inevitably occurring during a change of such a funda-mental character as that experienced by Kirkby families in moving out of Liverpool—the father's lengthened journey to work and the mother's involvement in a new home and new pattern of social activity. Recently juvenile delinquency in Kirkby appears to have declined and certainly today receives considerably less publicity than earlier. For this the police claim some credit for new and more efficient methods and these may well have combined with a number of other factors, including perhaps the many new outlets for adoles-cent energies now available. It may also be that the influence of the schools has been important: Kirkby comprehensive schools appear

1. For details of one school club see Mays, et al., School of Tomorrow.

sensitive to the need to provide the best from both middle-class and working-class traditions.[2] Certainly the town today contains many agencies of change which cannot fail to influence both adults and youth.

In addition to participation in more formal organizations, frequency of attendance or participation at football matches or other sports and visits to pubs, cinemas, or dance-halls was also obtained, again for pre-Kirkby days as well as the present. Sports and the pubs were currently the most popular of these, dance-halls the least. Cinema attendance at frequencies of more than once a month was low, but as Kirkby has no cinema of its own this involves the expense of a journey into Liverpool. In a survey of fourteen-year-old Kirkby schoolchildren,[3] it was found that the cinema took second place only to the school club in popularity and headed the list of amenities which their parents suggested were needed for the town. It is probable that although frequent attendance is rare, a high proportion of residents will attend occasionally.

Unlike participation in organized social activities, the number of Kirkby households with at least one member going more than once a month to one of the four forms of entertainment considered had gone down since the move in both samples. While in two-thirds of all households before moving some member went more than once a month, this proportion had decreased to about half afterwards (Table 50, Appendix A).

Frequency of attendance at sports and dancing appeared to show the least change, but the latter is in any case a minority occupation and probably in the main followed by the younger unmarried residents who are least affected by the length of journey required to reach a dance-hall. In both samples, the majority of those participating in one of these four activities did so outside the estate (Table 51, Appendix A). About half the attendances were made wholly outside while of the remaining half, some were made inside and some outside.

It is difficult to draw any general conclusions from these results: increased participation in more formal organized activities, decreased participation in some which are less formal and perhaps provide less opportunity for social interaction. Going to the pub and watching or participating in sports combine less formality with varying opportunity for interaction, and these, as we have seen, have remained popular. However, these results are complicated by the increased provision in the first case and decreased in the second,

2. Ibid. for an account of the way these problems are dealt with in one Kirkby comprehensive school.
3. Ibid.

and the apparent change may after all be simply accounted for in this way.

Generally, increasing affluence for the manual worker appears to encourage a more 'instrumental' attitude to work, resulting in increased interest in leisure activities. The type and quality of these certainly appear to be undergoing change throughout society and again the move to the estate would appear to provide an opportunity for new interests to replace old ones. Evidence from other studies, for example Sheffield[4] and Watling,[5] has suggested that generally formal associations are successful during the early years of an estate, when the difficulties of poor roads, lack of shops, and bad transport facilities bring people together in mutual aid or sympathy and so make them more ready to meet on a more formal basis. Often, however, the initial interest is lost, and if societies remain at all they tend to be taken over by small groups of people of a similar social standing. In Kirkby a gardening society was formed in West-vale in 1951 and became the most influential single group attached to the Community Centre there, its secretary eventually becoming secretary of the Centre. By 1952, however, the club had disappeared.

Kirkby has three community centres, one in each of the neighbourhoods, but at the time of the survey none had been completed although each provided meeting-rooms for societies. There is now a full-time organizer who supervises all the centres, and today most of the activities which take place there are for adults: they include keep-fit classes, gardening and other clubs, and a range of evening classes. Tennis courts are also available. These centres may not be used by a very large proportion of the population, but they do provide a focus and there is no doubt as to their success in catering for residents with a variety of minority interests.

On the face of it, it would not appear that opportunities for meeting socially or for taking part in organized activities are any less in Kirkby than in the city. However, it may well be suggested that equivalence is not sufficient and that to compensate for the move away from familiar places and people, more must be provided in the new than the old home. To some extent Kirkby has done this, and the facilities provided do appear to be used. One fundamental provision was lacking at the start, however, and was only beginning to reach a satisfactory level at the time of the survey—that is shops. It is unfortunate that these tend to be regarded by estate managers as merely places where goods may be bought and which may be temporarily replaced by mobile vans. They are undoubtedly the

4. *Neighbourhood and Community.*
5. R. Durant, *Watling, A Survey of Social Life on a New Housing Estate,* P. S. King and Son, 1939.

places where women tied by young children can meet others and eventually form a nucleus of acquaintances or at least of recognized faces.

Shops are rarely provided during the early years of a housing estate as it is not considered that there would be sufficient return to make them economic propositions. On the other hand, there is overwhelming evidence that this is an omission which hits the newly arrived resident hardest. It could be argued that there is as much of a case for subsidizing shops during the development of an estate as for the early provision of a community centre and social facilities.

CHAPTER 8

Conclusions from Kirkby

The Kirkby survey was made in order to see how far families moved from blighted areas of Liverpool to new estates outside the city boundary had been able to adjust themselves to a completely new environment. The background of one group of these people, the ex-Crown Street residents, had already been studied in detail and it was known that many living in the Crown Street area of Liverpool in 1956 had formed a strong attachment to it. In part this was due to a general familiarity, often going back for a number of generations, but in other ways it had more practical concerns. Good transport facilities giving easy travel to the docks or other centres of employment and plenty of shops selling at competitive prices were important facilities for people living on low wages and often with large families to keep.

Nevertheless, conditions of housing were such in this neighbourhood that one-third of its population in 1956 expressed a wish to move. It was particularly interesting here that the proportion doing so was highest in the area showing least movement in the past but an area which was beginning to show serious signs of physical and social deterioration as the cost of maintaining the property increased disproportionately to its value, while a move away became less and less easy as satisfactory accommodation at a rent that could be afforded became more difficult to find. It was also evident that those most willing to move were the young married people with children for whom they wished better conditions: modern schools, a clean and healthy environment, and space in the home. These are the people most likely to be found on the city's housing list and who have been moved to estates such as Kirkby, and it can be assumed that for a large proportion there could be few regrets at leaving their old homes.

Nevertheless, a willingness to leave does not necessarily lead to a readiness to accept whatever is substituted, and the impression left by Kirkby is that discontent was considerable. On this estate about one-third of the families expressed a wish to move away and only about one-half positively wished to stay. This pattern recurs in so many new housing estates where similar investigations have been made that it is important to consider how real, how lasting and how inevitable the objections of their residents are.

M.S.A.—6

Looking at the population of the country as a whole, since the industrial revolution people have become increasingly mobile until today there are few who have not had the experience of moving house at least once in their lifetime. Nevertheless, up to the beginning of the century for the majority of people movement over any substantial distance other than on marriage was generally made only for serious economic reasons. Since then, as public and private transport have developed, movement for the majority of families has lost its practical difficulties. Not only this, but communication over distances which at that time must have seemed immense is now of little consequence, and though after a move friends and relatives may live further away the distance must be considerable before contact need be broken. Today, more than half the population have moved house at least once over the previous ten years. More than half of those who do move do so primarily because they want to change their accommodation, and over the greater part of the country, three-quarters or more move less than ten miles.[1]

Thus although so many move, it would appear that most do not voluntarily make a break which will take them beyond the physical and social environment with which they are familiar. The long-distance move is still typically related to economic factors and may often be one which is otherwise not wished for. It would seem, therefore, that most people, and not only those from Crown Street, form ties with their immediate locality which are not readily broken, and that if they do change their place of residence entirely from choice they will do so in such a way that these ties may be retained even though reduced.

The general unpopularity of a long journey to work or a change of employment is undoubtedly a factor here, the former largely because of its cost financially and to a lesser extent its consumption of time. Commuting to work in the city from distant low-density localities has become more frequent in recent years, but mainly among those in occupations which carry a larger than average salary. As for changes of employment, for all except the young and un-attached these are not as straightforward as official encouragement might suggest.

The majority of people who move do so voluntarily, but the needs which they take into account operate to the same extent in those who have little or no choice as to where they are to live. The people living in Kirkby belong to this large minority, who not only can have little influence on when and where they shall go, but know that once the move has been made it will be difficult or even impossible to

1. A. Harris, *Labour Mobility in Great Britain 1953-63*, Government Social Survey, 1966.

move again, however unsatisfactory the new conditions turn out to be.

Since the provision of housing for those without the means to buy was accepted as a community responsibility, less than a hundred years ago, very large numbers of men and women have had the experience of a violent, and to all intents and purposes, enforced change of environment. When it means, as it so often does today, a movement out of the centre of cities, which have been the background of the families involved for many generations and the only known source of employment of the type required, however inadequately provided, it is obvious that such a change must produce a profound effect.

It might be expected that this effect would be greatest among people such as the Crown Street residents who had previously lived in closely knit communities with relatives nearby and associated in many ways with city life. The survey has shown, however, that there are few ways in which the ex-Crown Street group differ in their activities or attitudes to Kirkby life from other residents who may have moved in from very different areas in the suburbs, or even by exchange from other housing estates. The Crown Street sample's ties to the city do appear to be rather stronger: more are specific in their wish to return there, rather than merely to leave the estate. On the evidence of Bethnal Green and similar working-class communities it might have been expected that the need to keep closely in touch with relatives would also be an important factor here, but it does seem from the Kirkby survey that relatives, wherever they live, are regularly seen by a large proportion of all the estate's residents: the only difference found between ex-Crown Street residents and others in this respect was more contact between the former and siblings who live some distance away in the outer suburbs. There is some evidence, however, that for people from Crown Street attachment to relatives and acquaintances from their previous home is associated with their attitude to the estate, for those who believe they see their relatives less often than before and who say they have made few contacts locally, but have kept in touch with friends in Crown Street, are more likely than others to wish to leave Kirkby. This particular combination of attitudes did not arise in the case of residents originating from a wider area. A further distinction between the two groups arises in relation to the type of social contact made and may reflect some differences in custom. While visiting, or being visited, by nearby acquaintances occurred to much the same extent among both, the proportion of those from Crown Street who 'went out with' their neighbours, shopping or to some kind of entertainment, was much lower. More general attitudes to neighbours and feelings of loneliness or lack of privacy are displayed to much the same extent in both groups of Kirkby residents. The over-all impression left in looking at these and other groups of people of various origins who have been moved into municipal housing estates at various times is of unity of response.

If this is so, it might be said that these are the inevitable reactions of newly housed council tenants, and that time is the only remedy. That it is a remedy seems fairly certain. Estates such as Dagenham,[2] after similar periods of unrest, subside into acceptance. An older population with fewer young children to restrict and harass become familiar with surroundings and neighbours. Some vacated houses are taken by married children of early tenants. A redistribution of the residents has occurred, with a greater proportion locally employed.

Dagenham's early population contained as disproportionately high a number of unskilled workers as Kirkby does now. Twenty years later its structure reflected that of the region generally. Williams[3] reports that in 1937 in Norris Green, another Liverpool housing estate, later tenants were more likely to remain than earlier ones, and that the early tenants most likely to move away were those on the one hand finding rents too high either in conjunction with a long and costly journey to work or because they became unem-ployed, and on the other, those able to do better for themselves. He attributes the greater stability of these later tenants to 'better trans-port facilities, adequate shops, a demand for labour in the vicinity and perhaps a happier relationship between neighbours'.[4] Thirty years hence in Kirkby it is likely that, starting from conditions similar to those in the early Norris Green, the same processes will occur.

There is a good deal of evidence that the economic conditions of residents on an estate affect their general attitude to it. Cullingworth[5] reaches this conclusion after examination of a number of northern housing estates. It has been noted in Kirkby that although very few differences arise between the responses of ex-Crown Street and other residents, the former are slightly more attached to their old home. It is also the case that although the occupational structure of the two samples is very similar, three times the proportion in the Crown Street sample were unemployed at the time of the survey compared with the General sample. Long-term unemployment is a frequent experience in the Abercromby area of Liverpool where many of those in work are employed in casual labour, and it would seem that

2. Willmott, *The Evolution of a Community.*
3. *Problems of Population and Education in the New Housing Estates.*
4. Ibid., p. 48.
5. 'Dispersal—success or failure'.

the move to the estate had not improved their position as much as might have been hoped. Proportionately fewer of the Crown Street group also had been unable or unwilling to find work in Kirkby, though the proportion working in Liverpool was no greater. To be unemployed in Crown Street is bad enough, but to be unemployed in Kirkby, where little unskilled work is available and where one is seven miles from the centre of Liverpool, must lead to great difficulties. Perhaps the key to the widespread discontent lies in the words of an unemployed Kirkby waiter: 'This is a working-class community with a lot of unemployment. If it were more prosperous it would be better liked.'

In many New Towns now, including the north-west's own Skelmersdale, house-letting is tied to employment. In 1966 over 80 per cent of new Skelmersdale residents worked in the town. Nearly half of these residents had moved on account of the employment available there, as compared with less than one-fifth moving for work reasons in the country generally. The great majority had moved at least ten miles and nearly one-quarter had lived at their previous address more than twenty years—these at least were not among that group of people who tend to move at frequent intervals.[6]

Only 9 per cent of these people said that they were not pleased with their move. This is a great contrast to Kirkby, but it can be argued that the position of a New Town is quite unlike that of an overspill estate which has been developed specifically for people in housing need—people among whom are inevitably a high proportion of unskilled and unemployed who are hardly required by many new industries, if at all (unless they are women eligible for low wage rates). This is a dilemma difficult to resolve. Nevertheless, 30 per cent of Kirkby residents were working on the trading estate at the time of the survey compared with 10 per cent at the time of their arrival. There is, therefore, even here some possibility of a partial integration of home and work.

For the remainder, it might be expected that there would be quite a number ready to train for semi-skilled work on the estate if facilities were available. Some training is done at present by a few firms and some in government training centres, but the numbers affected are very small. Nevertheless, the number of centres is being increased and also the number of places at existing ones. Training might surely be encouraged, particularly among those now living in areas where the population is to be rehoused. There are those of course for whom it is unlikely that retraining is possible or wanted, and who are not likely to find work on or near the estates. It may be expected that their numbers will decrease substantially as a new generation with

6. *Population and Social Survey 1967*, Skelmersdale Development Corporation.

greater educational opportunities grow up. In the meantime, as redevelopment within the city is gathering speed it might be that such people could be given priority for the new central city dwellings.

Any sorting out or reorganization of this kind means additional work for the Corporation's Housing Department and is not likely to be a practical proposition without additional staff. Hilda Jennings, after a detailed study of Bristol residents before and after dispersal from the city to peripheral housing estates, lists as one of her recommendations 'achieving a local basis of employment', an objective which she considers of 'paramount importance'.[7] She suggests that a study should be made of the effects of the 'continued and accelerated separation of home and work place'. She also suggests the setting up of groups of local housing officers in the areas to be redeveloped, who can deal personally with problems of rehousing and become known as individuals to the families concerned.[8]

Such officers might also be the agents of the suggested distribution according to employment potentialities. If it were known that work would be available within easy reach for the chief wage-earner, this might go a long way towards reconciling families to the move. If in addition some real choice of accommodation by tenants themselves were possible, this would undoubtedly have a marked effect on their attitude to the estate. It has been shown in Kirkby and other estates[9] that those who have moved in by exchange and transfer are less likely to wish to leave than other residents. They have exercised choice and are therefore much more ready to tolerate inconveniences of accommodation or locality. Obviously such an arrangement would need an adjustment of rents between houses and flats. A substantial lowering of rent for the latter accompanied perhaps by some increase for the former might induce many more to take the flats.

It should be remembered that today provision of local authority housing is no longer a charity. Economic rents are widely charged, a reduction allowed only where there is a real need. The difference in value between the tax relief on a mortgage and the subsidy on local authority housing is often small. Council tenants are paying well for their houses and should not be criticized for expecting some consideration of their requirements.

Most housing estates, in spite of all the criticism, have much to recommend them to their new residents. Continually in Kirkby comments were made relating to improvements in the health of parents, children, or both since the move there. Eagerness to do what

7. *Societies in the Making*, p. 227.
8. Ibid., p. 228.
9. This was very evident in Halewood, another Liverpool estate, in which a survey was conducted in 1966 for Liverpool Council of Social Service: see Appendix D.

is best for their children is constantly displayed by parents in the redevelopment areas and on the estates, and they know that, educationally and physically, the new areas are superior. Typical of the attitude of many residents was the comment in Kirkby: 'It is a new way of life when we come here: we don't benefit but our children will.'

Given some observable concern for individual needs it might not be necessary to wait twenty years for an estate to 'settle down'. The New Towns appear to satisfy their residents with no such time-lag. In those such as Skelmersdale which link housing and employment, complaints appear less frequently. In the past City Housing Departments had little choice in placing tenants. Now that areas of dispersal are wider it is to be hoped that the new situation will allow greater flexibility and will be used to transform the character of new communities.

II MAGHULL

CHAPTER 9

The Maghull survey area

Maghull, the study area, lies in south-west Lancashire, eight miles north, and some twenty-five minutes drive, from the centre of Liverpool; it is four miles south of Ormskirk, four miles north-west of Kirkby, and some twelve miles south-east of Southport. Maghull is part of the City Region of Liverpool as defined in 1965 by the Liverpool City Planning Office, and part of the Liverpool Regional Hospital Board area. It lies within the area (Map 1) of significant commuter travel to Merseyside,[1] and within the area to which the large Liverpool department stores deliver goods most frequently. Maghull was included in the Joint Planning Board proposed by the Royal Commission on Local Government for the Merseyside Special Review Area in its report in December 1965.[2] The successor to this commission, the Royal Commission on Local Government 1966–9 under the chairmanship of Lord Redcliffe-Maud recommended in its majority report[3] that the study area should be included in the Merseyside Metropolitan Area; Mr D. Senior's 'Memorandum of Dissent'[4] assigned it to the Liverpool Region. The Commission, writing about the Southport/Crosby Metropolitan District in which it was proposed to include Maghull, stated that 'This district is increasingly becoming an area where people live who work in the Merseyside conurbation.'[5] Neither the majority report nor Mr Senior's report include Maghull in their proposals for a second tier Liverpool District: the former places Maghull in its Southport/Crosby Metropolitan District and the latter in Bootle District.

Maghull, which in 1823 was described as a 'pleasant village',[6] exists primarily as a result of its relationship with Liverpool, even though administratively it is still part of West Lancashire Rural District, and geographically it is still separated from Liverpool by

1. *Liverpool City Centre Plan*, 1965, p. 6.
2. *Report of the Royal Commission on Local Government*, Merseyside Special Review Area, 1965.
3. *The Royal Commission on Local Government in England, 1966–9*, Cmnd. 4040, H.M.S.O.
4. Ibid.   5. Ibid.
6. *Kaleidoscope*, 8 July 1823, quoted in the *Victoria History of the Counties of England: Lancashire*, ed. W. Page, vol. 3, University of London Institute of Historical Research, 1906–14, p. 215.

the River Alt and its water meadows, which in the past formed a formidable barrier.

The area taken for this study is that covered by the Maghull Town Map (Amendment 37, 1965, included in the Lancashire County Development Plan) and comprises the greater part of the parishes of Maghull and Lydiate (Map 3, p. 79). It has a natural housing boundary and, with minor differences, coincides with the area designated as a new urban district, with a population of 25,000 growing to 32,000 in 1981, in the draft proposals for the Merseyside Special Review Area of the Local Government Commission in their report in December 1965.

Both Maghull (Magele) and Lydiate (Leiate) are mentioned in Domesday Book, but the development of the area has been largely dependent upon and bound up with modern developments in transport—canal, railway, and road.

Early building, apart from scattered farms, was centred on the road from Liverpool to Ormskirk and the north, and another road which branches from this at the Maghull/Lydiate boundary towards Downholland and Halsall. The contruction of the Leeds and Liverpool Canal, which was proposed at a meeting in 1766 and which by 1774 linked Liverpool and Wigan, prompted a second stage of development. 'The upper end of Maghull village with its sett laid roads and gaily painted houses [formed] a typical canal-side settlement.'[7] The canal winds its way through present-day Maghull and Lydiate and forms a natural boundary in the south-east and north-west. The next stage of development came with the advent of the railway. There were two railway lines in Maghull: the Lancashire and Yorkshire line to Preston, and the Cheshire Line Committee railway to Southport (which has now been closed). Both form natural boundaries to the west and east of Maghull. Maghull station, now on the busy commuter line to Liverpool from Ormskirk, provided the nucleus of the next stage of housing development; the Victorian villas which lie to the west of the station are the only significant examples of Victorian building in Maghull.

At this stage in its development, Maghull's character was still distinctly rural. In 1901 Lydiate was described as 'chiefly agricultural . . . occupied by market gardens and fields where potatoes and cabbage alternate with wheat and oats . . . pastures are found principally in the low lying parts westward'.[8] Maghull was 'an agricultural township situated in flat country, fairly well supplied with trees, generally grouped about the village and farmsteads. The land is divided into arable and pasture, the latter mostly to the west, whilst numerous market gardens thrive on a light and sandy soil.'[9]

7. *V.C.H. Lancashire*, p. 215.　　8. Ibid., p. 201.　　9. Ibid., p. 215.

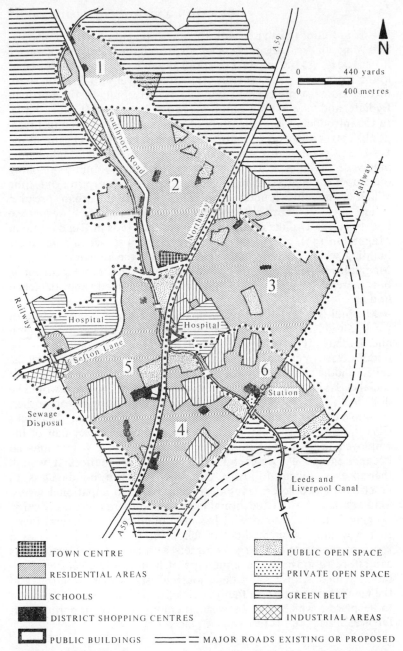

Map. 3. Maghull, showing the survey sub-areas: 1. Beechfield, 2. Lamb-shear, 3. Foxhouse, 4. Moorhey, 5. Broadwood, 6. Willowhey.

It was not until the 1930s, with the development of road transport, that Maghull began the process which gives it the suburban character it has today. As the city of Liverpool began to spread, development in the 1930s took place on either side of the Liverpool–Preston road, to the south; semi-detached bungalows were built to the north in Lydiate and along both sides of Moss Lane and Dodds Lane. In the introduction to their study of the Crown Street area of Liverpool Vereker and Mays describe the process, which was begun in the 1930s and continued in the post-war years, in which Maghull was involved: 'the cities . . . continued to increase their volume, stretching out into the countryside until by a process of absorption one time village communities found themselves engulfed in the urban spread'.[1]

Two areas of permanent council houses were built between 1950 and 1953, the Lydiate estate in 1950 and the Hudson Road estate in Maghull in 1952/3. 1955 saw the start of the post-war private sector building which has now almost covered all the remaining land in Maghull. Houses are mainly semi-detached with three bedrooms, but there is a minority of larger semi-detached and detached houses.

Maghull is essentially a place of residence rather than a place of work, although there are some small industrial estates in Maghull and Lydiate. It is suburban and it appears on the surface to be middle class. Yet the people who live in Maghull cannot all be called middle class in terms of any of the more traditional criteria of social class: in terms of occupation, education, or income it would be difficult to see what these people have in common with each other. A simple categorization by occupation using the Registrar-General's Classification of Occupations reveals that only just over half of the employed heads of households in the sample have a non-manual occupation and 43 per cent have a manual occupation. It would, therefore, be difficult to justify the use of the term 'middle class' to describe the people of Maghull as a whole in occupational terms. Similarly in terms of educational background there is great diversity, ranging from the lecturer who has just submitted his doctoral thesis to the window-cleaner who left school at fourteen but who as a result of capturing two large contracts with educational institutions can afford to move to the same type of house as the lecturer. Raymond Williams, discussing new housing estates, new suburbs, and the new towns, writes: 'in fact people of many different kinds live in these places, which also between themselves have important differences'.[2] Maghull is just such a place.

---

1. *Urban Redevelopment and Social Change*, p. 1.
2. R. Williams, *The Long Revolution*, Chatto and Windus, 1961, p. 331.

Yet Maghull people do have much in common with each other, and in order to justify the use of the term 'middle class' in the Maghull context we must look beyond simple objective classifications. Rosser and Harris in their study of Swansea define social classes in the following terms:

We think primarily of social classes in effect as broad economic divisions composed of individuals who recognize one another as peers; but they are also cultural groupings marked by distinctive standards and styles of living, and by characteristic values and social attitudes.[3]

It is the latter part of this definition which may be applied to Maghull; it is in the life which they lead in Maghull, rather than their backgrounds and occupation, that the people reveal their similarities.

Josephine Kloin suggests that 'House ownership and the residential area are, in affluent conditions, obvious criteria for class identification'.[4] The findings of Willmott and Young in 1960 add weight to this thesis: they reported that the figures for house ownership in Woodford among middle-class and working-class samples (self-ascribed social status) were 56 per cent and 36 per cent respectively;[5] and Rosser and Harris, using a much more subtle definition of class in their Swansea study, found that 75 per cent of the middle class, 64 per cent of the lower middle class, 53 per cent of the upper working class and 36 per cent of the working class were house-owners.[6] In 1966[7] 79 per cent of people in Maghull owned their house, compared with 50 per cent in Lancashire and 30 per cent in Liverpool. Thus if we accept house-ownership as a criterion of social class then Maghull is middle class.

The people of Maghull are middle class in their patterns of consumption rather than in terms of their relationship to the means of production. Another example of this is the level of car ownership. 68 per cent of the people in the Maghull survey area owned one or more cars, compared with 36 per cent for Lancashire and 28 per cent for Liverpool.[8] Similarly, in the Swansea study Rosser and Harris found that 59 per cent of the middle-class households had a car, 44 per cent of the lower middle class, 30 per cent of the upper working class and 18 per cent of the working class.[9]

The people of Maghull have, with their widely differing backgrounds and occupations, adopted middle-class consumption

3. C. Rosser and C. Harris, *The Family and Social Change*, Routledge and Kegan Paul, 1965, p. 95.
4. *Samples from English Cultures*, vol. 1, p. 424.
5. *Family and Class in a London Suburb*, p. 116.
6. *The Family and Social Change*, p. 106.
7. Sample Census 1966.
8. Ibid.
9. *The Family and Social Change*, p. 107.

patterns and middle-class values, and it is this which makes it possible to view Maghull as a whole as a middle-class suburb. This is the view taken by Rosser and Harris:

We have thought rather of our social classes primarily as broad cultural groupings—using the term 'culture' in the anthropologists' sense of a total style and manner of living, a way of life.[1]

The aims of the Maghull study were to look at the way of life in an area with this characteristic middle-class appearance. Two approaches were adopted. In the first place data relating to people in different areas of Maghull was compared—areas which previous to the survey were expected to show variation. In the second place the findings of the Maghull survey were compared with those of other studies of middle-class areas to discover whether any common pattern emerged which could be described as representative of a middle-class way of life, bearing in mind the warning which S. D. Clark puts forward:

In the very selection made of suburban communities for study however, a bias becomes built into the sociological conception of suburbanism. A high degree of order is found, characteristic of suburban society, but it is those suburban societies displaying a high degree of order which have tended to be selected for study and investigation.[2]

For the first approach, the survey area was divided into six sub-areas (Map 3, p. 79). There were marked physical differences among the sub-areas chosen, differences related largely to the time at which development in particular areas took place.

Sub-area 1, *Beechfield*, includes the old village of Lydiate, a district of scattered housing stretching along the old Liverpool–Halsall road, and also a number of small semi-detached bungalows built between 1932 and 1938. Having originated as a village it is still separated from the rest of the survey area by a stretch of open land; and it is administratively separate, being subject to Lydiate Parish Council rather than Maghull Parish Council, and is served by a general shop of the old village pattern.

Sub-area 2, *Lambshear*, also lies within the parish of Lydiate, but it seemed sensible to separate this from the other part of Lydiate since all the housing here, apart from a few houses along the Halsall road, were built in the post-war period. Housing is mainly semi-detached and privately owned, built after 1955, on an estate which straddles the parish boundary. There is also a small council estate built in 1950. The large shopping precinct for Maghull has been developed on the southern boundary of this sub-area and there are

1. *The Family and Social Change*, p. 112.
2. S. D. Clark, *The Suburban Society*, University of Toronto Press, 1966, p. 7.

plans to extend this in the next few years. Lydiate Industrial Estate, the site of four small firms, also lies in this area. Within the area is a primary school serving Sub-areas 1 and 2, and a Roman Catholic primary school which serves the whole of Maghull.

Sub-area 3, *Foxhouse*, is separated from Sub-area 2 by Northway, the four-lane dual carriageway road from Liverpool to Ormskirk and Preston. The preconceived idea that this was an important boundary in day-to-day life in Maghull was borne out during interviewing, when although no specific question was asked about it, several of those interviewed referred to the road as the 'Berlin Wall', an obstacle which was important to mothers and children in their everyday lives. Housing in this sub-area is mainly privately owned and semi-detached, built between 1959 and 1967; this is the most recently developed part of Maghull. Within its boundaries lie two primary schools, one a local authority school, recently opened, and the other the old Church of England school serving the whole of Maghull. A new Roman Catholic secondary school is being built in this area.

Sub-area 4, *Moorhey*, is contiguous with Sub-area 3, but it is separated from it by the Leeds–Liverpool canal. Again housing is predominantly privately owned and semi-detached but within the area lies the Hudson Road Council Estate which was built between 1952 and 1953 and on which about a quarter of the population of the sub-area live. The private housing is of two types: large semi-detached houses built between 1938 and 1939, and much smaller semis built on the edge of mossland by the side of the River Alt between 1937 and 1938. These latter houses cost considerably less than any other housing in Maghull. Fourteen of the 23 people in the sample with unskilled or semi-skilled occupations lived in this sub-area. Within it lies the Grammar School and a primary school built in the 1950s.

Sub-area 5, *Broadwood*, is separated from Sub-area 4 by Northway. The earliest development of Maghull in the 1930s took place in this sub-area. Most of it was built between 1930 and 1936 and the housing is predominantly semi-detached. There are, however, small pockets of post-war housing which fill in the gaps left by pre-war developers. Along the western boundary lies the Maghull Industrial Estate, which although small is expanding. The estate is separated from the housing by the now disused Liverpool–Southport railway. One of the two secondary modern schools in Maghull is found in this area; the other is on the other side of Northway in Sub-area 3.

Sub-area 6, *Willowhey*, has a distinctly different flavour from the rest of Maghull. It consists mainly of Victorian villas built around the railway station, but includes in addition a small development of mainly detached housing built in the late 1950s. There is a new primary school in this sub-area which was opened in 1967.

The statistical data presented in this study was derived from a random sample drawn from the population of the survey area in the spring of 1967. The sampling frame used was the electoral register for the electoral divisions of Maghull and Aughton within the parliamentary constituency of Ormskirk. The qualification date for inclusion was 10 October 1966, and the register included, in theory, all residents entitled to vote at the qualifying date. The survey was conducted over a period of two months, beginning in mid-May 1967. At the time of the survey, therefore, the register was between six and eight months out of date.

Since the sample for the survey was taken on a household basis, the difficulties created by deaths and people moving house were avoided. Where a new family had moved into the house, the new family was interviewed.

A sample of 286 households was drawn from the electoral register. So that comparisons could be made among the six sub-areas, the sample was taken as follows:

Sub-area	Sampling fraction	No. of house-holds selected
1. Beechfield	1 : 6	45
2. Lambshear	1 : 45	47
3. Foxhouse	1 : 42	48
4. Moorhey	1 : 27	47
5. Broadwood	1 : 33	47
6. Willowhey	1 : 9	52

In 245 households the interview schedule was completed, representing a response rate of 86 per cent; 11 per cent of the households refused to complete the interview schedule, and in the remaining 3 per cent no contact was made.

Since at the time the study was made the investigator was himself a resident of Maghull, he was also involved as a participant observer and much of the data additional to the survey data was collected in this way.

CHAPTER 10

Geographical and social mobility

Whilst Census data can be only of very limited value in studying geographical mobility, it may be useful to take as a starting point a comparison of data from the Maghull survey with Census figures. In 1961 11 per cent of the population of England and Wales had lived in their present residence for less than a year and 34 per cent for less than five years. In Maghull, however, the incidence of movement was less: 6 per cent had lived in their present house for less than one year and 29 per cent for less than five years.

Figures of this kind must of course be related to the context of the area. It is important in considering residential mobility to relate length of residence in the present house to the length of time the house has been standing. This is particularly relevant in an area like Maghull where there is a large proportion of comparatively recent development, and where as a result the vast majority of the people who had lived in Maghull for only a short period of time had nevertheless lived in their particular house for the full lifetime of the house. Even where the householder is not the original occupier, it is important to discover whether or not he intends to stay in that particular house for a long period of time or whether he intends to be a short-term householder. Census data cannot tell us why people move, how far they move, or indeed who the people are who are moving.

It seems clear, however, from a comparison of figures that Maghull is an area of low residential mobility. One of the two estate agents with offices in Maghull said that he relied heavily upon the other suburban areas in south-west Lancashire and upon older property in north Liverpool to make his business profitable. It was impossible, he said, to run a profitable business based on Maghull alone because so few houses come on to the market.

There are very few people in Maghull who fit into Watson's 'spiralist' category: Watson defines 'spiralism' as

the progressive ascent of . . . specialists of different skills through a series of higher positions in one or more hierarchical structures, and the concomitant residential mobility through a number of communities at one or more steps in the ascent.[1]

In his study of neighbours, H. Bracey found that nearly 50 per cent of private estate dwellers expected to move, and in an overwhelming number of cases the reason given for the move was job transfer. For all but two of the 36 per cent of his sample who had previously lived in distant towns the move had involved removal of more than eighty miles.[2] In Maghull, however, only 22 per cent of the sample gave employment as their reason for having moved to Maghull, and many of these had not moved because of job transfer but because they were already employed on the industrial estates at Aintree, Netherton, and Kirkby and wanted to live near to their work. Sixty-three per cent on the other hand said that it was the house and/or the area which attracted them to Maghull (Table 54, Appendix A). Maghull is very like S. D. Clark's notion of the stereotype of the American suburb which he criticizes as the home of the 'other directed organization man'. He suggests that:

For the population moving to the suburbs only one quality gave distinctiveness: the need for the kind of housing the suburbs provided. What general characteristics the suburban population possessed were related, directly or indirectly, to the fact that it was the search for a house which determined the move to the suburbs.[3]

Further evidence indicating that the people of Maghull do not fit Watson's 'spiralist' category comes from their answers to a series of questions about future geographical mobility. Only 5 per cent of the sample had any definite plans for moving from Maghull (Table 57, Appendix A). Seventy-two per cent said they had no wish to move, and of those who did express a wish to move only about one-sixth (5 per cent of the whole sample) gave considerations of employment as their reason (Table 56, Appendix A). Most of those who wished to leave Maghull wanted to move to one of the other suburban areas in south-west Lancashire—Southport, Ormskirk, or Formby.

People who move to Maghull have not, on the whole, moved very far: only 14 per cent of the sample had lived more than forty miles from Maghull in their previous residence (Table 55, Appendix A). On the other hand only 3 per cent of the sample were true 'locals' in that they already lived in Maghull before moving to their present house.

---

1. W. Watson, 'Social mobility and social class in industrial communities', in *Closed Systems and Open Minds*, ed. M. Gluckman, Oliver and Boyd, 1964, p. 147.
2. H. Bracey, *Neighbours*, Routledge and Kegan Paul, 1964.
3. *The Suburban Society*, p. 83.

Fifty-eight per cent of the sample had moved to Maghull from the Liverpool conurbation (Table 55), most from north Liverpool. From a geographical point of view this group too could be described as 'locals' since Maghull is part of the Liverpool conurbation. This does not mean, however, that the move to Maghull has no significance for these people. Rosser and Harris talk about local names serving as banners of class distinction: Maghull, for Liverpool people, is just such a 'verbal banner'. For these ex-Liverpudlians Maghull and the place they come from are, from the social point of view, miles apart.

If instead of looking at the residents of Maghull in terms of their previous residence we look at the places in which husband and wife variously spent their youth a similar pattern emerges. Just over four-fifths of both males and females in the sample households had been brought up within forty miles of Maghull and 63 per cent of the males and 60 per cent of the females had spent their youth in the Liverpool conurbation (Table 58, Appendix A). Again the move to the suburbs for these people would seem to have been a stepping-stone to higher social status rather than part of the series of geographical moves which the 'spiralist' might make. William H. Whyte suggests that:

in part these communities are a product of the great expansion of the middle class, for the new suburbs have become a mecca for thousands of young people moving up and out of city wards.[4]

People of this kind make up a much higher proportion of the population of Maghull than they do of the areas which Whyte was looking at.

The move to Maghull for many of these people was the realization of an ambition. One woman, who like her husband had spent her youth in Bootle and had rented a terrace house in Bootle when she married, put it in these words:

When we got married we decided we would save hard so that we could move out to Maghull or Formby. Now we are here we are here to stay. Why should we want to move away? We've got everything we want.

In a study of the Crown Street area of Liverpool it was found that one-third of the young couples in the sample wished to move to the suburbs to 'better themselves'.[5] Many of the people in Maghull see themselves as having fulfilled this wish: they too wanted 'a house with a garden, or a modern house, or one which would be dry and have a bath, hot water or a lavatory indoors'.

4. William H. Whyte, *The Organization Man*, Simon and Schuster, 1956, p. 246.
5. Vereker, *et al.*, *Urban Redevelopment and Social Change*, p. 101.

There are, of course, some spiralists in Maghull: a town with new private housing within striking distance of large industrial complexes such as Kirkby and Netherton two or three miles away, and Liverpool itself only eight miles away, is bound to attract professional and managerial workers without roots. They are, however, small in number, they are not typical of the residents of Maghull and these families tend to be acutely unhappy during their stay in Maghull. As an accountant put it:

People just don't want to know you. They are all Liverpool people who have friends and relations in the area. They don't need us. My wife tried to get a coffee and baby-sitting circle going, as she had done in our previous house, without any success. We can't wait for the time when my firm moves me again.

The sub-area which showed the highest proportion of spiralists was Foxhouse, the area with the newest housing development, but even there they formed a very small minority. From remarks made by some of the people interviewed it appears that the spiralist does not usually look for a house in Maghull but prefers to live on the coast at Southport or Formby or 'on the other side' of the Mersey. Maghull, then, is largely a suburb for the people of Merseyside; its population, once it has invested in the purchase of a home, becomes to a high degree a settled population.

Whilst Maghull is not the home of the spiralist, one of its distinctive characteristics is that it is a home for the socially mobile: this came out time after time in the interviews. Even where no occupational mobility was apparent, particularly in the case of people from Liverpool, the feeling was expressed that the purchase of a house in Maghull was the achievement of an ambition.

If a conventional definition of social mobility as inter-generational movement from a manual to a non-manual occupation is used, a two-way table (Table 18) is produced. It is clear that in these terms the majority of people were not mobile socially (51 per cent), and that

TABLE 18

*Social mobility of heads of household
in Maghull—two-fold*

		Father's social class	
		Non-manual	Manual
Respondent's	Non-manual	20%	36%
social class	Manual	13%	31%

36 per cent were upwardly socially mobile and 13 per cent were downwardly socially mobile.

However, this two-fold classification into 'manual' and 'non-manual' is not really adequate for analysing occupational mobility for it fails to take account of significant movements within the two groups, such as the clerk's son becoming a teacher or the labourer's son becoming a foreman. Continuing with the definition of inter-generational occupational change, it is possible to use a finer occu-pational classification than the straightforward manual non-manual division. For this purpose the Registrar-General's classification of five 'socal classes' is used, with an additional distinction between people in 'social class' III with non-manual and manual occupations (Table 37, Appendix A) Using this six-fold classification Table 19

TABLE 19

Social mobility of heads of household in Maghull—six-fold (percentage of sample)

Respondent's social class	Father's social class					
	I	2	3	4	5	6
I	0·2	0·2	1·4	6·5	0·7	0·7
2	0·3	3·6	2·5	7·7	1·4	—
3	—	2·8	9·1	12·4	5·1	1·4
4	0·7	2·3	8·0	16·9	4·2	2·0
5	—	0·7	1·4	0·5	3·0	3·3
6	—	—	—	—	0·8	0·1

is produced. In this case all those household heads to the right of the boxes have been upwardly mobile with respect to their fathers and those to the left have been downwardly mobile. Those lying within the boxes have been socially immobile. This means that half of the sample have been upwardly mobile with respect to their fathers, 17 per cent have been downwardly mobile, and a third have not been mobile.

This approach has been used by many of the major studies of social mobility, such as those by Glass,[6] Bendix and Lipset,[7] and

6. D. Glass, *Social Mobility in Britain*, Routledge and Kegan Paul, 1954.
7. R. Bendix and S. M. Lipset, *Class, Status and Power*, Free Press of Glencoe, 1963.

Miller.[8] Yet the idea that social mobility is to be understood purely in terms of occupational change raises serious doubts. Apart from obvious difficulties such as father and son being at differing places on their career lines, there are more important weaknesses highlighted by Colin Bell:

Individuals can rise or fall in terms of nation wide, or even international bureaucratic hierarchies, not only industrial and productive but also educational, political, religious, etc.; or of local communities.[9]

Certainly for many people living in Maghull, it is in terms of movement in the local community, in this case Liverpool and its environment, that they have been socially mobile. The move to Maghull for many residents of 'downtown' Liverpool, Bootle, or Walton represents a move to higher social status whether or not it involves a change in class position in occupational terms.

Looking now at the six sub-areas of Maghull, two of these—Lambshear and Broadwood—would appear at first sight to have attracted the (occupationally) downwardly mobile person. The survey data shows, however, that in both these cases downward mobility meant in the main a one-category movement in the six-category classification: in Lambshear 7 out of the 10 who had been downwardly mobile, and in Broadwood 8 out of 10, had moved down only one category. It would therefore be wrong to assume that there is some special feature about these areas which attracts the downwardly mobile. All other areas had roughly the same proportions of the downwardly mobile; and no area appeared to attract the upwardly mobile or the occupationally immobile any more than the others.

It would seem from this that each of the sub-areas, despite differing appearances, serve the same kind of function in attracting people to Magull. Moorhey with its lower-priced housing attracts the largest proportion of people with low occupational status; and Willowhey with the highest proportion of detached housing attracts the highest proportion of people with high occupational status.

What is interesting is that people in all sub-areas tended to give the same reasons for moving to Maghull; that they liked the area generally and that the area offered them the sort of house they wanted to buy.

8. S. M. Miller, 'Comparative sociability', *Current Sociology*, xix, no. 1 (1960).
9. C. Bell, *Middle Class Families*, Routledge and Kegan Paul, 1968, p. 47.

CHAPTER 11

Social life

Much has been said in recent years about the stripping of the family's functions in the industrial society, including the loss of the social functions of the family. In considering the social life of the people of Maghull, two aspects seemed particularly important. In the first place it seemed relevant to consider the social life of the nuclear family living in Maghull, and secondly to consider the place of the extended family in this field.

Only 10 per cent of the household heads worked in Maghull. Nineteen per cent worked on the industrial estates at Kirkby and Netherton; 56 per cent worked in Liverpool and Bootle; 4 per cent worked somewhere else in Lancashire, and 5 per cent had an occupation which involved travelling in one form or another (Table 59, Appendix A). So, for a large majority, home and workplace were separated by distance, and as a result the daytime lives of husband and wife were separate. Like Mr and Mrs Matthews, whose daily round is described by Willmott and Young in their study of Woodford,[1] the wife spends her daily life on the estate and the husband is removed from the family situation during his working hours.

Most husbands spent the rest of the day and the weekends with their families. Only two husbands in the sample fitted the absentee husband stereotype of 'the executive who spends nearly all his time out of the home not so much spending money as making it';[2] but many husbands spend one or two nights a week working overtime to supplement the family income. In the main, however, Maghull husbands spend much of their leisure time with their families, and most of this leisure time is spent in the home. S. D. Clark points to a similar situation in his Toronto study:

The suburban was a society built around the family group. What was different about this society from the old established urban society was the extent to which the energies of the whole population were concentrated upon the single interest of establishing a home for the family. This interest was uppermost in determining the structure of social life that developed. Almost everything the new suburban resident found himself doing, within the suburban setting and in the world outside, was related to the

1. *Family and Class in a London Suburb*, pp. 17 ff.
2. Ibid., p. 20.

needs of the family . . . Within the new suburban community thus it was scarcely possible to speak of a society outside that of the family. People lived the whole of their lives—almost—within the family group.[3]

Ronald Fletcher, arguing against R. M. MacIver's view that recreation was one of the non-essential functions of the family which has been increasingly replaced by the provision of recreational facilities by outside agencies such as clubs and cinemas, quotes Mark Abrams's comment: 'It is primarily in the home that the worker now has his greatest opportunities of exercising and enjoying his craftsmanship.'[4]

There are, of course, in Maghull and its surroundings, many opportunities for recreation outside the home, and people do make use of this provision; but the over-all picture of social life in Maghull is of spasmodic use of outside facilities rather than massive, full-time use. The general picture is of home-centred recreation; people are not seeking a new social life when they move to Maghull—they are seeking a home.

Husbands in Maghull spend less of their leisure time in the home than do their wives. Table 20, compiled from the replies of all the

TABLE 20

Number of evenings spent at home during the week prior to interview

No. of evenings spent at home	Husbands %	Wives %
7	42	55
6	25	28
5	15	9
Less than 5	18*	8
Not known	1	1

* This includes 5 per cent of the total where the husband was away from home the previous week for employment reasons.

families where there was both a husband and wife, shows that 13 per cent of husbands and 8 per cent of wives were away from the home voluntarily for more than three evenings in the week previous to interviewing.

Television, which has been variously pointed to as the reason for the decline in support of recreational provision outside the home, provides the home itself with a centre of recreation. Only eight of

3. *The Suburban Society*, p. 191.
4. M. Abrams, article in *The Listener* of 26 November 1959, quoted by R. Fletcher in *Family and Marriage in Britain*, Penguin Books, 1966, p. 197.

the households in the sample (5 per cent) did not have a television (Table 61, Appendix B). Four of these were people over the age of sixty, three of whom were widows; the other four were in their thirties and forties, and all were in the Registrar-General's non-manual class III.[5] Of the eight household heads, four never went to the cinema, three went rarely and one went once a month.

Of the television owners, two-thirds had watched television on the evening prior to interview, and nearly three-quarters said that they watched television every day. Of those who had watched television the previous evening approximately equal numbers had watched BBC I, ITV, or both, and only 5 per cent had watched BBC 2 exclusively (Tables 62 and 63, Appendix B).

In the course of his argument about the recreational functions of the family, Ronald Fletcher poses a series of unanswered questions:

Do families never gather at the end of the day around the fateful face of television? Do they not argue over the respective merits of Wagon Train, Sunday Night at the London Palladium, Tonight, the Brains Trust? Are they not irritated by Bronowski and charmed by Ayer?[6]

Certainly in modern Maghull the previous evening's television programmes provided a popular topic of conversation, at least with the interviewer. Television emerges as an important feature in the recreational lives of the people here.

There is one cinema in Maghull, the Albany, part of a small chain which includes the Everyman Theatre in Liverpool and two or three small cinemas in Liverpool and Wallasey. The owner was unwilling, for reasons of confidentiality, to give precise attendance figures, but he commented:

Cinema audiences have steadily gone down from the peak year of 1957, each year, up to this year [1967] when they have shown a slight increase. But the attendance rate is very bad indeed in comparison with the peak of 1957.

He further suggested that there is a weekly pattern in cinema attendance:

the Mondays, Tuesdays and Wednesdays of the week could almost be put aside, they are so small, and we only start taking any money on the Thursday, Friday and Saturday, escalating each day. We could in fact close the first half of the week, I am quite sure, and we should not suffer very much, if at all, for the capacity of the cinema could easily accommodate all Monday, Tuesday and Wednesday takings in any one night at the latter end of the week.

5. See Table 37, Appendix A.
6. *Family and Marriage in Britain*, pp. 195-6.

Liverpool, with its great variety of cinemas, particularly in the central area, is a much greater attraction for cinema-goers, despite a poor bus service. With two-thirds of the households in the survey area owning at least one car, and with a half-hourly train service, transport into the city centre, some eight miles away, is no difficulty for most people.

Less than one-fifth of the sample can be regarded as regular cinema-goers, in that they go regularly once a week (Table 65, Appendix B). Nearly two-thirds of these made their weekly visit to the local cinema in Maghull, but for all other people the majority of cinema visits had been to one of the Liverpool cinemas. The people who visited the Maghull cinema tended to live in the sub-areas closest to the cinema. Twenty-one per cent of the sample never visited the cinema at all, and 63 per cent of cinema-goers who went at least once a month said that they had no preference as to which cinema they visited. As one man put it, 'You go to see a film, not to sit in your favourite cinema.'

Maghull people, then, do not spend a lot of time at the cinema. They spend even less time at the theatre. Less than 1 per cent of those interviewed had visited the theatre in the week prior to interview, 6 per cent had visited the theatre in the previous month, and 43 per cent said that they never visited the theatre. Typical of the rest were those who made an annual visit to the theatre to see a show or a pantomime as part of the Christmas ritual.

Seventy per cent of the sample were not members of any clubs, a level of non-membership which is similar to that of the working-class section of the Willmott and Young sample (66 per cent) and very much higher than that among their middle-class group where non-membership was 48 per cent.[7] This reflects the general social apathy which was directed towards organized recreation by the people of Maghull, and also the lack of organization and amenities of this kind in Maghull. It is difficult to say whether greater provision would lead to greater participation or whether this lack of partici-pation is an expression of the suburban resident's wish to be left alone. Replies to a question asking what people thought about entertainment in Maghull (Table 74, Appendix B) suggests that a greater provision would lead to greater participation: 77 per cent of the sample were dissatisfied with the provision. They expressed a wish for more entertainment, but they were not themselves willing to organize it, a feature which perhaps reflects their predominantly working-class tradition. Fewer people (54 per cent) expressed dis-satisfaction with their own social life (Table 74, Appendix B), suggesting that there were many people who were satisfied with a

7. *Family and Class in a London Suburb.*

non-public social life centred around the home and friends. This tends to reinforce the argument that people do not move to Maghull for the social life it offers but rather because they want a home of the kind which is offered in Maghull.

The gap in organized social activity is partly filled by two thriving evening centres: according to estimates given by the two principals of these centres, about one-fifth of the adult population attended classes in the session 1967-8. The actual figure is likely to be a little below this since no allowance was made for attendance by an individual at more than one class per week, but it remains a high one.

The two major centres are the two secondary schools in Maghull, one on either side of Northway at Deyes Lane and Ormonde Drive. The centres offer, to quote the prospectus, 'a balanced programme of activities for the rapidly expanding population of Maghull';[8] in addition, 'it is hoped that activities will develop in classes of a social nature'.[9] A wide variety of activities is offered and some of the groups have indeed gone beyond the usual social life which is to be found in the classes. To quote one of the principals:

From members of classes in previous years a number of independent groups have been formed which still function in and through the Centre although they have their own committees and programmes. These groups comprise the Maghull Motor Club, Maghull Art Group, Maghull Scottish Society, Maghull Camera Club, and a badminton club. Through these groups a very lively social side to the centre activities is maintained and the building is used every evening and many weekends.

Some of the classes cater exclusively for women—women's keep fit, dressmaking, floral art—and others exclusively for men—men's keep fit and keep fit (older men), but most of the classes are available for both sexes although there seems to be a tradition that some are male pursuits and others female pursuits. In 1967-8, for instance, while woodwork and golf were both mixed classes, car maintenance had an all-male clientele and typewriting was all-female.

Two-thirds of those attending the classes in 1967-8 were female. It appears that the classes are catering predominantly for the wife on the estates and predominantly for adults. The principal of the second centre said that it was difficult to find non-vocational classes which attract the under twenty-ones.

Evening classes in Maghull are, however, becoming increasingly popular year by year. The number enrolling in the 1967-8 session showed a 20 per cent increase on the numbers in the previous session. Average attendance was very high, around 90 per cent at both

8. *Prospectus*, Further Education Centres, Maghull, Lancashire Education Committee, Division 11, 1966-7.
9. Ibid.

centres, suggesting that the centres are filling a gap left by the lack of voluntary provision of such amenities in Maghull.

There are nine public houses in the survey area, varying in character from an old coaching house on the Liverpool–Halsall Road to the modern chromium-plated public house. In just under a half of the households in the survey the husband had been to a pub during the week before the interview took place, and a little over a half had been to a pub at some time during the previous month; one-quarter of husbands never went to a pub (Table 64, Appendix B). These figures compare closely with those quoted by Kessel and Walton who found that 47 per cent of males visit a pub at least once a week and 22 per cent do not drink.[1]

The choice of the 'regular' pub was one of the few features covered by the survey where significant differences were found between sub-areas. Each sub-area tends to have its own 'local', and regular drinking patterns established themselves on a local basis related to the positioning of the public house. Beechfield contains only one pub, and 8 out of the 11 regular male drinkers in the sample used this pub. There are three pubs in Lambshear: an old coaching house, an old canal-side pub, and a pub rebuilt in contemporary style in the 1950s. This last pub is the local for the residents of this sub-area: 15 out of 21 regular male drinkers drank there whilst the other two pubs attracted only 3 of the regular drinkers. Both of these other pubs serve largely as out-of-town drinking places for Liverpool people.

Foxhouse has two pubs. One was built, together with the housing around it, between 1954 and 1956. It is modern in style and attracted 18 out of the 26 regular drinkers in the sample from this sub-area (Foxhouse was incidentally the sub-area with the highest proportion of regular drinkers amongst its inhabitants). The other pub here is not so much a local as an out-of-town pub. It, too, is modern in style, but caters mainly for a male clientele and has 'super-attractive' barmaids. The Everton football team used this pub as a rendezvous and this perhaps partly explains why it attracts people from all over Liverpool. Only 4 out of the 26 regular male drinkers in Foxhouse used this pub regularly.

Moorhey has one pub, built before the war and situated next door to the local cinema. The Broadwood sub-area begins just across the main road from here, but only 2 out of the 21 regular male drinkers in Broadwood used this pub, whereas 9 of the 18 in Moorhey were regulars there.

Broadwood has one pub in the centre of the sub-area, and there

1. *Hulton Readership Survey*, compiled by J. Hobson and H. Henry, 'Alcoholism', Hulton Press, p. 49.

are two others just outside the boundary in Moorhey and Lamb-shear. Ten of the 21 regular male drinkers in the Broadwood sample drank outside Maghull, a larger proportion of non-Maghull drinkers than in any other sub-area. Four of them went to Ormskirk and four into Liverpool, in each case to a public house which had been a 'local' before the man in question had moved to Maghull. Four of the 21 visited the central pub regularly and 6 went to one of the two pubs on the outskirts of the sub-area in Moorhey and Lambshear.

Willowhey has only one pub, next door to the railway station. Eleven of the 16 regular drinkers interviewed here used this as their local.

In general, then, the public houses serve a local area, or at least the people of Maghull tend to select one of the public houses in their own sub-area to serve as their local. In all the sub-areas except Broadwood there is a public house which serves this function. Other public houses in the sub-area, where there are any, seem to attract people from outside Maghull, and provide primarily for Liverpool people, especially at the weekend. There is of course some crossing of sub-area boundaries in the choice of 'usual pub', but by and large the boundaries of the sub-areas chosen are significant in this parti-cular aspect of social life. Only 15 per cent of the regular male drinkers went outside Maghull for their regular drink, indicating that Maghull itself is the centre of operations for men who like a regular drink.

So far we have looked only at male drinking habits in Maghull. In just under a fifth of the households in the sample the wife visited a pub regularly at least once a week, and just under a third went at least once a month (Table 64, Appendix B). Forty-three per cent never went to a pub, comparing with 40 per cent of the women in the Hulton Readership Survey.[2]

Less than 7 per cent of the women visited a public house regularly, and when they did it was usually with their husbands at weekends. This was particularly a feature of households without children or where the children were growing up. For these weekend visits the 'pub in the country' was more likely to be chosen than the local Maghull public house.

Seventeen per cent of the women in the sample visited a public house regularly. Less than 7 per cent of the women said they had a 'usual pub' and when they did so, it was usually one that they visited with their husbands at weekends. Regular drinking, it appears, is part of a man's world, but occasional drinking, especially at the weekends, is part of the joint lives of husbands and wives.

In looking at social life outside the home, it seemed worthwhile

2. *Hulton Readership Survey*, 'Alcoholism'.

to consider two other activities which tend to provide exclusively for one sex—these were football and bingo. If husband and wife live separate lives in their leisure time it would seem reasonable to expect a large following in these spheres.

In the homes where there was a husband, about two-thirds did not watch football regularly; 20 per cent were regular supporters of Liverpool Football Club, 11 per cent were regular supporters of Everton, 2 per cent claimed to support both, and a further 2 per cent regularly supported some other team (Table 67, Appendix A). Football, then, was an important part of the leisure-time lives of 35 per cent of the men for about two-thirds of the year, although most of these regular supporters only watched home games, not travelling long distances to watch their team playing away. Since most of the interviewing was done in the football closed season, there was little evidence in the interview situation of absentee husbands on a Saturday afternoon.

One would not expect, perhaps, to find a large bingo following amongst wives in a middle-class area, but since many of the Maghull families were migrants from Liverpool, and since bingo sessions were run by the local cinema and by the Roman Catholic Church apart from many centres in Liverpool, it semed that bingo might possibly play a significant part in leisure activities in Maghull. However, in the households where there was a woman 86 per cent never went to bingo, and only 4 per cent went regularly, once a week or more (Table 66, Appendix B). The local cinema manager talked about this lack of support for bingo:

With regard to bingo at Maghull, we tried this ourselves and it was a failure, but from October 1st this year [1967] we leased Sunday nights to a company who are trying once more with bingo, and it is much too early to say how they will progress.

The men of Maghull, then, spend some of their leisure time away from the family, but for the women there is very little independent social life. The evening centres provide one outlet for women; the social side of church life provides another. Women use the social provision of the church slightly more than the men: 93 per cent of the men in the sample made no use of the social side of church life, compared with 84 per cent of the women who played no part (Table 68, Appendix A). Eleven per cent of the women in the sample attended a mothers' union, women's fellowship, young wives' group or some similar organization; this was the only type of church social activity which received any real support. Typical of these organizations is the Young Wives' group of the Parish Church of St Andrew. The group meets fortnightly, the meetings lasting about

two hours, and attendance during 1967 varied between thirty and
forty. A typical year's programme included a variety of activities:
a trip to a flour-making factory; talks on many subjects including
fire prevention and haematology; a hairdressing and cookery
demonstration; and, quoting one of the women who attended,

about two or three religious type meetings per session—for example, the
other week the vicar talked about his year's exchange with an American
vicar. A couple of months ago, a vicar's wife talked on *A Child Questions
God.*

The session lasted from September till June and at Christmas a joint
carol service was held with other young wives' groups from neighbouring parishes in west Lancashire. Members of the group took it
in turns to provide tea and cakes for the rest of the group.

Support for the thesis that Maghull is middle class in its way of
life comes from the survey data on church attendance. Carr Saunders, Jones, and Moser suggest that 'Frequent church going becomes
markedly less common with decline in the social scale',[3] and David
Martin says: 'Suburbs appear to be places of relatively high practice,
and they are the only areas outside traditional market town or
country districts where Anglicanism recovers some of its dominance.'[4]
Peter Willmott in his study of Dagenham found that 83 per cent of
the population never went to church,[5] and in Peter Townsend's
study of old people in Bethnal Green, he found that only 13 per
cent attended in the course of a month.[6] These two studies showed
that church attendance in working-class areas tends to be much
lower than in middle-class areas. Willmott and Young found that
34 per cent of the middle class in Woodford had attended church the
previous month while only 17 per cent of the working class had
attended in the same period.[7] Table 21 shows that the level of church
attendance in Maghull is closer to the level among the Woodford
middle class than among the working-class groups quoted above.

Church-going, like so much else in Maghull, is essentially a family
affair: 96 per cent of the men and 88 per cent of the women who
went to church regularly went with their family.

The nuclear family, then, is the most important social group in
Maghull and it has a dominant influence on the way in which leisure
time is spent. Most leisure-time activity is family activity, and this is
highlighted by the way in which families spend their week-ends.

3. A. M. Carr Saunders, D. C. Jones, and C. A. Moser, *Social Structure of
England and Wales*, Oxford University Press, 1958, p. 261.
4. D. Martin, *A Sociology of English Religion*, S.C.M.P., 1967, p. 47.
5. *The Evolution of a Community*, p. 140.
6. P. Townsend, *The Family Life of Old People*, Routledge and Kegan Paul,
1957; Penguin, 1963, p. 142.
7. *Family and Class in a London Suburb*, p. 63.

TABLE 21

Church attendance in Maghull

Frequency of attendance	Men %	Women %
Attended within previous month	28	31
Not attended in previous month but go to church	15	19
Never go to church	57	50

Week-ends, for the people of Maghull, are the time when one has a real choice in leisure, and at week-ends it is the family which takes precedence. Families shop together on Saturdays, visit friends and kin together at week-ends, go for car drives together, particularly on Sunday afternoons, garden together, and usually watch television together on both Sunday and Saturday evenings.

CHAPTER 12

Social contact with the extended family

Talcott Parsons's argument that only the isolated nuclear family is functionally consistent with the occupational system and the structure of contemporary society has been challenged in recent years by several studies in both Britain and the United States. Eugene Litwak, after carrying out a survey of wives in the Buffalo urban area, suggested in two articles[1] that a modified form of the classical extended family can exist in a mature industrial economy despite the effects of physical and social mobility, because improvements in communications can overcome the effects of spacial separation. Stacey,[2] Willmott and Young,[3] Rosser and Harris,[4] and Bell[5] have shown that the extended family is still important, even for the middle class. The modified extended family, defined by Litwak as 'a series of nuclear families joined together on an equalitarian basis for mutual aid, not bound by demands for geographic propinquity or occupational similarity',[6] certainly has importance in the lives of Maghull families. The findings of the Maghull survey support the findings of other studies in middle-class areas, with certain variations which are a product of the particular area in which Maghull lies. Rosser and Harris make the point that:

First towns differ, and industrialism has a variety of characteristics—a simple point, which is as important as it is obvious . . . There is considerable variation of social system from one urban area to another . . . We cannot assess the wider applicability of the conclusions of a particular study until we have a full and detailed picture of the particular social environment in which the study was undertaken.[7]

Since Maghull is, to all intents and purposes, a suburban extension of Liverpool, and since a majority of Maghull people have their

1. E. Litwak, 'Occupational mobility and extended family cohesion' and 'Geographic mobility and extended family cohesion', *American Sociological Review*, xxv, 1 and 3 (1960).
2. M. Stacey, *Tradition and Change*, Oxford University Press, 1960.
3. *Family and Class in a London Suburb.*
4. *The Family and Social Change.*   5. *Middle Class Families.*
6. E. Litwak, 'The use of extended family groups in the achievement of social goals', *Social Problems*, vii (1959), 178.
7. *The Family and Social Change*, pp. 28 and 29.

origins in Liverpool, it would be possible to argue that the move to Maghull only represents a move within a restricted locality, and that this ought to make relationships with kin much more easy to continue. It is clear, however, as argued before,[8] that the move to Maghull for most of the people with their origins in Liverpool is much more than this. For the Liverpool people, as for non-Liverpool people, Maghull is a 'long way' from their families of origin, socially if not geographically.

The study revealed that 85 per cent of the households consisted of nuclear families, that is to say they consisted of husband and wife, together with children if any. Ten per cent were incomplete nuclear families, including the widowed and the single; and a further 6 per cent had at least one permanent additional member from outside the nuclear family living in the household (Table 52, Appendix A). In about half of these the additional member came from the family of origin of the householder or his wife, and in the others, the additional member or members were the families of the children of the householder. Colin Bell[9] in his Swansea study found that one in ten households had a permanent additional relative outside the nuclear family as a member; in Maghull the proportion was slightly smaller.

Bell found in his study that there was no difference in the geographical distribution of wife's parents when compared with husband's parents; the Maghull sample was similar in this respect (Table 22).

TABLE 22

Proximity of married subjects to parents

	Husbands	Wives
Parents living:	%	%
Within 15 miles	68	72
Within 80 miles	10	8
Over 80 miles	22	20

Rosser and Harris reported that in Swansea in 1965 only 20 per cent of all married sons and 15 per cent of all married daughters lived more than twelve miles from their parents.[1] In the 'middle-class' part of the sample, 28 per cent of married sons and 32 per cent of married daughters lived more than twelve miles from their parents; and the figures for the 'working-class' group were 17 per cent of married sons and 10 per cent of married daughters. The

8. See p. 90.   9. *Middle Class Families.*
1. *The Family and Social Change.*

figures for the Maghull sample (32 per cent of married sons and 28 per cent of married daughters living more than fifteen miles from their parents) resemble closely the 'middle-class' part of the Rosser and Harris sample, but they differ sharply from the results of Colin Bell's study. He found that 56 per cent of the married sons and 67 per cent of the married daughters lived more than twelve miles from their respective parents. He goes on to say, however, that 'these differences are obscured if "same locality" is broadened to western Swansea and the twelve mile cut-off point is extended to twenty-five miles'.[2] The area in which a particular study is carried out has an important influence in this respect, and while generalizations can be made about middle-class life, the results of a study must always be looked at in terms of the geographical and social environment in which the study took place.

Peter Townsend's definition of the extended family depends upon daily or almost daily contact:

The extended family may be said to consist of a group of relatives comprising more than the immediate family, who live in one, two or more households, usually in a single locality, and who see each other every day, or nearly every day.[3]

Defined thus the extended family hardly exists at all in Maghull. In order to consider relations with the wider family in Maghull we must think of the extended family as a social entity and not define its form precisely, for in defining its form it is possible to overlook something which has social significance.

In the Maghull sample just over half of the families had at least one member of both sets of parents still alive; 71 per cent had at least one member of one set of parents alive and in only one-quarter of the cases were both sets of parents dead. As might be expected, it was in the older-established sub-areas, where the householders also tended to be older, that there was the highest proportion of couples whose parents were dead. Fifty-six per cent of the householders in Beechfield and 60 per cent of the householders in Willowhey had no parents left alive, while in the newest sub-area, Foxhouse, where in the main the families were in an early stage of the family cycle, the proportion was only 16 per cent. When it came to visiting those parents who were alive, however, the differences between the sub-areas disappeared.

All weekly and daily visiting between parents and their married children was confined to those parents and children who lived within fifteen miles of each other; and all daily visiting was between parents

2. *Middle Class Families*, p. 79.
3. *The Family Life of Old People*, p. 108.

and children who lived in the survey area, with one exception where the parents lived at Old Roan, Aintree, about two miles from Maghull, on a direct rail and bus route. In all the cases where the parents lived on the Wirral, on the other side of the River Mersey, contact was on a monthly basis. Geographical mobility will obviously affect the amount of physical contact between members of the extended family, but as Colin Bell suggests, 'There seems to be no reason why it should result in a lessening of ideological and emotional commitment to kin and/or disrupt relations between kin altogether.'[4]

Married sons and daughters visited their parents more frequently than the parents visited their children (Table 23). This was a universal

TABLE 23

Frequency of contact with parents (married people with parents alive)

	Husband's parents		Wife's parents	
Frequency of visits	*Family visit parents*	*Parents visit*	*Family visit parents*	*Parents visit*
	%	%	%	%
Daily	2	2	8	4
Weekly	36	22	43	35
Monthly	30	14	22	17
Occasionally (less than once a month)	33	62	27	44

pattern, true for all the sub-areas, for all occupational classes and no matter what the physical distance was between parents and children.

There was more contact between the Maghull family and the wife's parents than there was between the Maghull family and the husband's parents (Table 23). When these figures are broken down by occupational social class of the Maghull family, it appears that the higher the class of the Maghull family the stronger is the link between the husband's parents and the Maghull family and the weaker the link between the wife's parents and the Maghull family, measured in terms of direct contact between them. The obverse is true: the lower the class of the Maghull family, the stronger is the link with the wife's parents and the weaker is the link with the husband's parents.

Another finding from the Maghull survey, for which the evidence is based on casual comment during the interviews recurring suf-

4. *Middle Class Families*, p. 86.

ficiently often to be worth mentioning, was a phenomenon which could be called 'suburban schizophrenia'. This occurred in those families with working-class backgrounds from the poorer areas of Liverpool who themselves had not experienced social mobility in occupational terms. These people had made the move to Maghull by dint of hard saving and in many cases long hours of overtime to enable them to buy the Maghull house. During the week these families lived a life which on the surface was no different from that of their neighbours, but at weekends there was a tendency to return to their families of origin on both Saturday and Sunday, but especially Sunday, where they became temporary members of a different way of life and played roles quite different from the roles they played during the week.

Brothers and sisters, too, are important in the extended family. Each household which was visited was asked to make a detailed list of the place of residence of both husband's and wife's sisters and brothers and the frequency with which they were visited. Over half of all siblings lived within fifteen miles of Maghull; 12 per cent lived between fifteen and eighty miles away and 29 per cent lived more than eighty miles from Maghull.

In comparing these figures with those for the residence of the parents of Maghull householders and their wives (Table 22), it is clear that brothers and sisters have moved further afield—only 22 per cent of husband's parents and 20 per cent of wife's parents lived more than eighty miles from Maghull.

The siblings of the Liverpool-born part of the sample showed a strong tendency to live in the Liverpool area; few lived in Maghull. Six per cent of all siblings lived in Maghull and Lydiate. The wife's sister was more likely to live in Maghull than were any of the other categories: 13 per cent of wife's sisters lived in the survey area compared with 3 per cent of husband's brothers, 4 per cent of husband's sisters and 3 per cent of wife's brothers. Sixty-one per cent of all siblings living in Maghull were sisters of the wife of a Maghull family.

There were 730 siblings listed by the families interviewed, and in all but twenty-two cases there was reciprocity in the frequency of visiting. This contrasts with contact with parents where it was found that parents visited their children less frequently than children visited their parents. If the Maghull family visited the sibling once a month, then the sibling usually visited the Maghull family once a month.

Two features emerge from Table 24: first, contact between the Maghull family and its female siblings is more frequent than contact with its male siblings; secondly, the relationship between two

TABLE 24

Frequency of contact with siblings
(siblings of married people in sample)

Frequency of contact	Husband's siblings		Wife's siblings	
	Brothers	Sisters	Brothers	Sisters
	%	%	%	%
Daily	1	3	1	6
Weekly	10	13	19	26
Monthly	9	23	12	28
Occasionally (less than once a month)	80	62	69	40
Number of siblings	160	213	155	202

sisters, at least in terms of frequency of contact, was much stronger than any of the other relationships between brothers and sisters. It would seem then that the female determines relationships between siblings.

Willmott and Young found a similar pattern in the Woodford study,[5] although it appears that day-to-day contact between siblings was stronger there than in Maghull. There was also more frequent contact between married men and their brothers than was evident in the Maghull sample. The Maghull sample was closer to the middle class in Woodford than it was to the working class. In Maghull 80 per cent of the siblings had not been seen in the week prior to interview; in Woodford 79 per cent of the middle-class and 75 per cent of the working-class siblings had not been seen in the same period,[6] a statistically significant difference.

The extended family, then, is an important social unit for the people in Maghull, contact with parents being more important than contact with siblings. Measuring frequency of contact as an indicator of the structure and function of the family may be inadequate because it ignores contact by telephone and letter, and cannot discover the level of kinship sentiment, but it gives a strong indication that the extended family is by no means a dead institution for the middle class, despite the lack of day-to-day, face-to-face, contact.

5. *Family and Class in a London Suburb*, p. 171. 6. Ibid., p. 170.

CHAPTER 13

Friends and neighbours

The extended family is still important for the people of Maghull, but friendship is also an important factor in their social lives. Except in unusual circumstances the one does not replace the other or prevent relationships with the other from flourishing; instead the two coexist and complement each other.

William H. Whyte writes:

> On the surface the new suburbia does look like a vast sea of homogeneity, but actually it is a congregation of small neighbourly cells ... Propinquity has always conditioned friendship and love and hate, and there is just more downright propinquity in suburbia than in most places.[1]

Friends are important to two aspects of social life in Maghull. In the first place they are important to the family life which both husband and wife share; secondly, they are important to women who meet their friends in the home (men tend to go out to meet their friends, particularly to the public house). In both cases, but especially in the latter, neighbours were the most important source of friends.

Half of the sample had regular weekly meetings with friends in their home, and 82 per cent met friends at least once a month in their home (Table 69, Appendix B). The importance of the home-centred, family-centred life of people in Maghull can be seen here: in 60 per cent of the contacts husband and wife visited or were visited together (Table 70, Appendix B).

Most of the friends lived locally. A quarter of the contacts were between people living in the same road and just over a third were with people living elsewhere in Maghull. Only 14 per cent of the contacts were with people from the home town of the Maghull family; it seems that friendship patterns emerged within the context of Maghull, rather than persisting from the pre-Maghull residence (Table 71, Appendix B).

Clark in his Toronto study suggests that people do not move to suburbia deliberately seeking a new social life:

> People settled where they found the house that they wanted. Friends and acquaintances might be found nearby, but if they were it was more by accident than by design. House buyers had been too interested in finding

1. *The Organization Man*, pp. 303–4.

the type of house that they could afford to be concerned about the preservation of social associations of the past.[2]

This description sums up the attitude of the people interviewed in Maghull. For the most part they were not seeking to preserve friendships from their previous life, although these friendships did exist, nor did they deliberately seek out new friends. Friendship grew from daily contact with people, whether this contact was with neighbours, workmates, or with other mothers taking their children to school.

Neighbours, and particularly neighbours who are friends, have replaced kin in the day-to-day needs of families. As Mogey has said, 'Mobility creates neighbours in the place of kindred.'[3] It appears, however, as Colin Bell has suggested, that this replacement is only superficial. 'Superficial' is perhaps a misleading word, for what appears to have happened in Maghull is that neighbours have partially replaced the extended family. The sphere of social relationships has widened: instead of many functions being fulfilled by the extended family, some of these functions have been taken over by friends. What Bell is trying to suggest is that even for the middle classes the extended family is still a functioning institution; in the Maghull context this certainly appeared to be so.

Whyte in his study of Park Forest said: 'We went into every other factor that could provide for friendship patterns ... Just as the resident had said, it was the layout that was the major factor.'[4] Physical proximity was the most important single factor governing friendship in Maghull: 31 per cent of the friendships mentioned by members of the sample were products of 'being neighbours' (Table 72, Appendix B). Another 28 per cent, however, arose as a result of contact at work; in all but 10 of these 106 friendships this work contact was reinforced by common residence in Maghull, but the fact remains that in these friendships a common workplace was as important a factor as common residence. Other considerations are of course at work in creating any friendship—common attitudes, shared interests and values which provide the stimulus for friendship. Whyte's statement seems therefore rather too sweeping to fit friendship patterns in Maghull, but physical proximity nevertheless emerges as the central factor in the making of friends.

2. *The Suburban Society*, p. 140.
3. J. Mogey, a private communication quoted by J. Klein, *Samples from English Cultures*, op. cit., p. 131.
4. *The Organization Man*, p. 314.

CHAPTER 14

Shopping

An analysis of shopping patterns was made from survey data and observation in an attempt to illustrate the different levels at which people live their lives in Maghull. Shopping at the manifest level is a necessary way of providing oneself with the necessities and luxuries which one requires, but at a latent level it is a means of social inter-action. Without overstressing this latter aspect of shopping, it appears that shopping is important socially to (1) the wife who spends her day at home, and (2) the family, for weekend shopping in Maghull is largely a family activity. This analysis of shopping patterns reveals the reliance which a suburb like Maghull has upon Liverpool, but also stresses the fact that day-to-day life in the suburb is largely self-contained, at least for the women.

Each sub-area has its own local shopping area, very much in the same way as each sub-area has its local pub. These two aspects are perhaps, together with friendship choice, the only aspects of life in which the locality is important; these are the fields of social relation-ships in which the lives of men and women are separate. In nearly all other respects Maghull people of different sub-areas live similar lives. In this respect too life in one sub-area is very much the same as life in another, but here at least the locality is the sphere of operations.

Beechfield has five shops, two of which were empty at the time of the survey. The three occupied shops were a general grocer's of the old village type, a newsagent and tobacconist which also serves as a sub-post office, and a small supermarket. Four of the houses in the area on the main Liverpool–Halsall Road had at one time served as shops but they had been bricked up and turned back into houses long before the survey took place, some time since the last war. It is reasonable to assume that these shops were opened when the new bungalow development took place in the 1930s but closed down because there was insufficient support when the rest of Maghull began to be developed and the motor car brought other shops within striking distance. The shops which existed at the time of the survey provided for the daily needs of the residents of the sub-area: 32 of the 38 housewives in the Beechfield sample usually shopped there from Monday to Friday, 30 of them using these shops regularly for their groceries.

In Lambshear there was the Central Square shopping precinct, which served those people living nearby in Lambshear and Foxhouse for local shopping but which also, as we shall see later in the chapter, served as a central shopping area for the whole of Maghull. Within this sub-area there were two other major local shopping areas and a third development of six shops built at the same time as the Coronation Road housing development; these shops were still unoccupied some ten years later, presumably because the local shopping provision in the area was already more than adequate. Both of the two functioning shopping areas in Lambshear are large and offer a variety of services.

Foxhouse has two shopping areas, one of four shops built to serve the houses constructed in the 1930s around Dodds Lane, and a row of fourteen shops built in the 1960s to serve the extensive housing development in the sub-area. The former consisted of a greengrocer/grocer, a draper's shop, a newsagent/tobacconist, and a small self-service grocer's shop. The other shopping area, on Eastway, contained a much wider variety of shops.

Moorhey has two major shopping areas, the first on Moorhey Road, serving the council-owned estate, and the other on Dover Road, serving the privately owned estate. Whilst Dover Road served the private development for its everyday needs, it also served the whole of Moorhey with its sub-post office and the whole of Maghull with its electricity and gas showrooms. Two other groups, each of four shops and both situated on service roads of Northway, complete the provision in this area. One of these comprises a tobacconist, café, ladies' hairdresser, and a bank, and the other a newsagents and tobacconist, a pet shop, a ladies' hairdresser, and a draper.

Shopping provision in Broadwood is extensive, along both sides of Liverpool Road South. There are really two groups of shops separated by about 200 yards of housing but it seems sensible to regard this as continuous shopping provision along both sides of the main road; although for the people living beyond the extremes of the shops one section only serves as a local shopping area. There is another group of shops in Broadwood which in 1967 had recently been vacated. These were on Holmfield Road and consisted of a supermarket, a sweet shop and tobacconist, a draper's shop, and a ladies' hairdresser. The opening of the Central Square shopping precinct about a quarter of a mile away was said to have made business deteriorate to such an extent that these shops were likely to remain empty.

In Willowhey there are nine shops, scattered in two groups along Station Road. The first group, which consists of shops built at the time of the Victorian development around the station, includes a draper's which also serves as a sub-post office, a chemist, a butcher, a hardware shop, and a grocer's. The other group consists of wooden huts occupied by a tobacconist, a decorator who also sells drapery, and an electrician, and a brick-built newsagent and tobacconist shop.

The provision of central shopping in the new Central Square precinct is supplemented by a group of older shops which were originally part of the canal-side development in the late eighteenth century. All but two of these shops provide central services and cannot be looked upon in any way as local shops. They include a bank and estate agent in a new building, a general store which is open on Sundays, a seed- and corn-merchant who also sells pet food and fishing tackle, a ladies' and gents' outfitter, a tobacconist, and a large do-it-yourself store.

More than half of those interviewed thought that shopping provision in Maghull was good, a third thought it reasonable, and the remainder considered it poor (Table 74, Appendix B). The people who lived in Beechfield and Willowhey, however, were less enchanted with local shopping than people in the other sub-areas: only 8 out of 38 in Beechfield and 18 out of 47 in Willowhey rated it good. These two sub-areas were not as well provided for as the rest; the new development in Maghull had largely passed them by and in consequence so had new local shopping.

In considering the social functions of shopping, it must be borne in mind that during the daytime husband and wife lead separate lives. The husband's daily life is centred upon the workplace and in the main the wife's is centred upon the home. Three-quarters of the families in the Maghull sample were at the child-rearing stage of the family life cycle, and for the wives in these families in particular shopping was a most important means of establishing social contact with other wives. Although no questions were specifically designed to explore this aspect of shopping, time and again in the course of the interviews the wife would indicate the importance of shopping as part of her daily round. Many said that they went to the local shops every day, not because they really needed to buy something but in order to meet people, or perhaps 'because Mrs X up the road called in on the way to the shops so I went with her for the company'.

Meeting friends at the shops seemed to be such an important part of these women's lives that a close look was taken at one of the local shopping areas, that on Eastway in Foxhouse. On any day when it was not raining the shops and the broad pavement fronting them were a thriving place for social contact. Some women arrived at the shops alone, many would come in groups of two, three, or four, probably with pram or push-chair. The women who were alone when they arrived would inevitably stop to talk, they would pass from one group to another and would carry out their shopping as they did so. There was great fluidity in the groups: a group of women would arrive together, would then break up when they arrived at the shops, would join and leave other groups talking on the pavement, and would regroup an hour or so later for the journey home. It was clear that the local shopping centre was an important gossip centre of which the shop assistants were an integral and important part. Many of them were part-time workers who lived in the houses surrounding the shops and appeared to act as 'central clearing-houses' for gossip.

The most clearly observable example of this was the super-market. From Monday to Friday progress was very slow through all but one of the checkout desks; here there was no gossip just a concentrated effort to keep people moving. The choice was left to the customer: those who simply came to buy goods used the fast desk, the others queued and talked at the slower desks.

The whole atmosphere in the supermarket changed about four o'clock on a Friday, and a new regime operated through Friday evening and Saturday. Father accompanied wife (and children) and the car-parking space outside the shops became inadequate; at any other time of the week there was plenty of room to park a car. On Friday evening and Saturday buying became the only important occupation, and the assistants who would talk incessantly during the week would now greet the people they normally chatted to at length with a 'Hello' and perhaps a few words only.

Shopping on Friday evening and Saturday by Maghull residents is a family occasion. The husband is home from work with his car, making it possible to shop further afield than at the local shops. Nine per cent of the sample went to Ormskirk on a Saturday morning for their week-end groceries; although only four miles away, Ormskirk does not feature in the weekly shopping patterns of the wives. During the week the push-chair, the pram, the children, or the lack of a car mean that the geographical limits of the wife's world are set in the locality. The presence of the car and its driver extend the limits at the week-end as far as Liverpool and Southport (Table 25).

The 'Monday to Friday' figure in Table 25 for the Central Square shopping precinct includes 18 out of 40 people in Lambshear who use these shops as their local shopping area because it is close to their homes. If the table is amended to include these people in the 'Local shops' category, the figures would read: Local shops 88 per cent, Central Square 15 per cent. These figures for shopping are another illustration of one of the central features of life in Maghull: during

TABLE 25

Usual shopping place

Place	Monday to Friday %	Saturday %
Local shops	75	40
Central Square	28	41
Liverpool	3	17
Elsewhere	5	12

Note. Some had more than one usual shopping place for a given part of the week.

tho daytime In the week husband and wife live separate lives, but at week-end life centres around the family.

The shopping context also illustrates Maghull's reliance on Liverpool. There are no department stores in Maghull, only two men's wear shops, two dress shops, one furniture and carpet shop, and one Woolworth's. Any shopping which caters for more than the everyday family needs must, therefore, be done elsewhere. Ninety-one per cent of the sample shopped in Liverpool when they wanted to buy clothes and 95 per cent for furniture; furthermore, Maghull lies in the zone of maximum delivery by the large Liverpool department stores. Southport provides the only other important shopping area for items such as clothes and furniture: 13 per cent of the sample bought clothes in Southport and 6 per cent bought furniture there.

CHAPTER 15

Maghull as a community

Colin Bell, discussing the difficulties of research into family life in suburbia, quotes a statement made by Molly Harrington:

the variety and range of family and neighbourhood patterns found in the newer districts may be seen less as a tangled web to be unravelled than as an example of the diversity of human behaviour when the rigid framework of physical necessity is loosened and personal choice is a major determinant of life style.[1]

The most striking thing which came out of the Maghull survey, however, was the remarkable similarity of life styles and attitudes in the six sub-areas which were selected. Although people in no sense feel that they belong to Maghull in the way inhabitants of a village feel part of the village, they live very similar lives to one another, and this despite a variety of backgrounds and life-experience. It is reasonable to suspect that this uniformity stems from a desire to conform to a pattern of life which people feel is expected of them when they come to live in this particular area. There is nothing tangible which brings the people of Maghull together as a whole, nothing which makes them feel that they belong to Maghull: there is only observable similarity.

Bell suggests, in summarizing the macro-ecological approach to the study of suburban social relations, that

it can be argued that the prices of the houses act as a social sieve with graduated meshes as it were, through which drop each homogeneous segment of the population round the edges of towns.[2]

This does not seem to provide a satisfactory explanation for the remarkable homogeneity of life in Maghull. For instance, although owner-occupied houses account for the vast majority of housing in Maghull, prices vary considerably from the very lowest semi-detached prices in the Liverpool area (there are a few terrace houses at even lower prices) to expensive detached houses. The majority of houses are admittedly three-bedroomed semi-detached houses, but there is sufficient variety of housing to expect a variety

1. M. Harrington, 'Resettlement and self image', *Human relations*, xviii (1965), 136.
2. *Middle Class Families*, p. 129.

of people from different backgrounds. R. Pahl suggest that 'there is a tendency in England at the moment for people to move to estates which are dominated by people of similar socio-economic status'.[3] The evidence of the Maghull survey shows that, as far as occupational categories are concerned, the variety of housing does indeed attract a variety of people and that it is on reaching Maghull that they become homogeneous. It is reasonable, therefore, to assume that the similarities in the way in which Maghull people live their lives is a product of living in Maghull and is not part of some predetermined selection procedure based on house prices.

The majority of Maghull people come originally from Liverpool; they move to Maghull to become 'middle class' (regardless of occupational class) or to remain 'middle class'. The non-Liverpool people move there because it provides the sort of housing which they would choose in whatever town they moved to. All these people have an expectation of the sort of life they will lead in Maghull and this is reinforced or modified by the life which they find actually going on there. The style of life which this combination creates could be called 'middle class', but there are differences between the sort of life which is found in Maghull and that which is found in other 'middle-class' areas. The style of life to be found in Maghull is a subtle mixture of a common suburban life to be found throughout the country, and local characteristics and expectations, in this case largely dictated by immigrants from Liverpool.

The type of social relationships which are to be observed in Maghull do not appear to fit the sequential hypothesis of social relationships suggested by Mowrer,[4] who describes life in suburbia as going through four stages: (1) home-centredness; (2) primary group neighbourliness; (3) individualization; (4) community relations. Dobriner in his study of Levittown suggested that

As the years went by, however, and as families moved away and new ones took their place, the early solidarity and spontaneous cliquing gave way to greater formality and social isolation.[5]

It is very difficult to see Maghull in general in these terms. Its development has taken place over a long period of time and different parts of Maghull have developed at different times; while it is possible to see something of the sequence in some parts of Maghull, it is really necessary, in using such an approach, to study the development of social relationships from the beginning, and this is not practical in

---

3. R. Pahl, 'Class and community in English commuter villages', *Socialogia Ruralis*, v (1965), 19.

4. E. R. Mowrer, 'Sequential and class variables of the family in suburban areas', *Social Forces*, xl (1961).

5. W. M. Dobriner, *Class in Suburbia*, Englewood Cliffs, N.J., 1963, p. 136.

a place which has grown over such a long period of time. The great value of this approach is that it is dynamic and can serve to show that different groups behave in different ways. What is important in Maghull is that there was no evidence, even on a small scale in the older parts of Maghull, let alone in Maghull as a whole, that the residents had turned their interests away from the primary group to the wider community.

There was primary group neighbourliness in both the old-established and the newer parts of Maghull; but there was also social isolation. The two things coexist and seem to have little to do with length of residence. There are friendship patterns and contacts with kin, but for most people Maghull in its wider sense has no social significance.

The majority of the sample—nearly three-quarters—said that they 'felt they belonged to Maghull'. An interesting feature was that in Beechfield 27 out of 38 suggested to the interviewer, without prompting, that they belonged to Lydiate rather than to Maghull. Evidence indicated, however, that 'belonging to Maghull' was not an expression of any kind of social belonging to a community: it was rather an expression that they were able to live the sort of life, in this piece of suburbia, which expressed their self-feelings about status. Maghull was important in that it was not Liverpool; Lydiate was important in that it was not Maghull.

Membership of the Ratepayers' Association gives a better guide to commitment to the community than does a simple question about belonging to Maghull. Only a quarter of the sample were members, the majority coming from Lambshear and Foxhouse, the newer areas—areas which in Mowrer's hypothesis should not yet have reached a stage of commitment to a community. The Ratepayers' Association was the only apparently successful community organization in Maghull, so judgement as to the level of community feeling can only be based upon the evidence of this one association.

The Association was comparatively recent in its origins. It was born in Foxhouse and its original objectives were to improve facilities on the large new estate in that area. Membership dwindled as the short-term objectives were achieved; since it broadened its aims to cover Maghull as a whole membership has increased but its members are largely non-participant.

In December 1967 the Association held a meeting at the Meadows Hotel in order to look into 'the facts and fancies and possibilities of erection of a civic hall'.[6] The meeting was well publicized and representatives of all local organizations were invited to attend.

6. Maghull Ratepayers' and Residents' Association, *Newsletter*, January 1968.

The outcome of the evening was, to say the least, disheartening and disappointing ... Some Associations left at half time ... The meeting failed to realize [or didn't wish to realize] that the Ratepayers' Association wished others to join them ... in such a venture.[7]

This incident highlights the residents' lack of interest in anything which concerned Maghull as a whole. It could be that this lack of community orientation stems from the fact that there are very few 'locals' in Maghull; Bell[8] makes the point that in Swansea it was the locals or burgesses who had the greatest commitment to the community. The vast majority of people in Maghull are committed to the home and to the primary group, and to a small circle of friends, but are entirely uninterested in any group with a broader base. These are the associations which command their loyalty, and beyond this few Maghull residents would seem to find need or justification for any further involvement.

7. Ibid.   8. *Middle Class Families.*

III KIRKBY AND MAGHULL

CHAPTER 16

Constraints and choice in Kirkby and Maghull

The type of accommodation and the residential area in which a household lives is the result of an interaction of constraints and choices dependent upon factors within and outside its control.

Income is the basic constraint which operates on all but a few, although the proportion of income which it is considered reasonable to allocate to accommodation will vary from one household to another, as will the form in which that allocation is made— mortgage, rent, or other financial arrangement. One criterion of 'middle-class' behaviour is a greater tendency than among the working classes to take account of the future, to take out life insurance policies, for example, or make regular savings. On this basis, taking out a mortgage on a house is more likely to appeal to middle-class than to working-class attitudes, while renting a house is similarly more in key with a traditional working-class outlook. Considerable variation between households in the operation of this constraint is possible, when all its aspects are taken into account.

Other constraints will depend upon the particular economic or social circumstances of the household. Economic constraints secondary to income will include the availability of suitable employment for the wage-earners, and today this must often mean employment for the wife as well as the husband. Availability is again a very flexible term. To the man who can afford to buy a car and use it for the journey to work it can relate to a far wider area than it does to the man who must rely on public transport. To this extent the more affluent salaried man is most free of this particular constraint, though such a man may be more restricted when he looks for a firm or institution which will give him the job and perhaps the opportunity for improvement which he wants. Here such constraints may often force him to move long distances as his requirements become more and more specialized, while the majority of manual workers, in normally prosperous times, are in this respect more free.

Social factors will depend largely upon the type of household and the stage in its life cycle which it has reached. Children of pre-school, school, and post-school age will each constrain their families through their need for facilities such as clinics, schools of a type or standard considered adequate by the parents, and provision for further education or employment. Needs of the retirement period will differ from those of middle age, local shops are important to some people, a rural environment to others. Clearly these are not independent factors but each may provide its own contribution to the total constraining force and each will influence the individual's satisfaction in or rejection of the situation in which he finds himself. Such forces provide an infinite number of combinations which become apparent when a decision to move is made.

Nevertheless, it is only at the position of extreme constraint, where poverty and other adverse conditions combine, that some element of choice of accommodation is not available. The extent of choice will vary according to the strength of constraints but again there is no simple relationship between the two, for the specific choice that is made will reflect the life style considered appropriate or adopted by the individual or family concerned.

While constraints are closely related to class—for those which are strongest depend very greatly upon economic factors, and so upon the occupation followed by the family's chief wage-earner—choice is related to status in that it reflects the household's patterns of consumption as well as its aspirations.

Kirkby and Maghull illustrate clearly the ways in which certain constraints and choices take effect, for the constraints which operate on many of their residents are the same. Both areas are, above all, places for young families with young children: 88 per cent of Kirkby's household heads and 71 per cent of Maghull's were less than fifty years old. The proportion of complete and incomplete nuclear families and extended families was exactly the same, but although the modal number of family members was four in either case, there was a far higher proportion of families with six or more members in Kirkby, and while the mean family size in Maghull was 3·5, in Kirkby it was 4·9. Both these are higher, however, than Liverpool's 2·8 and the mean of 2·9 for England and Wales.

In their ties with Merseyside too, they are remarkably similar. Slightly more than 60 per cent of Maghull's husbands and wives spent their childhood in Liverpool, and about three-quarters of Kirkby parents were born there. For employment, they almost equally rely on the conurbation.

Occupationally the differences are more distinct, though perhaps the proportion of non-manual workers in Maghull, less than 10 per cent greater than the proportion of manual workers, is not as high as many would expect in such an area. Maghull gains in professional and managerial workers while Kirkby gains in the semi-skilled and unskilled, but the proportion of skilled manual workers is only a little less in Maghull than Kirkby, and this occupational group is the one most highly represented in both areas. Perhaps therefore it is within this group that the differences in life style which distinguish Maghull and Kirkby should be examined.

Gans[1] sees class and life cycle stage as key characteristics associated with the basic patterns of urban structure, yet this group (the skilled manual workers), which accounts for just over a third of the households in each area, would generally be considered of the same class, and the great majority will be at the same stage in their life cycle, living as a nuclear family in which there are children of school and pre-school age.

Intra-class distinctions which affect aspirations and life style have been recognized by Margaret Stacey[2] in Banbury and Mogey in Oxford.[3] Stacey sees a division between 'traditionalists' and 'non-traditionalists' which cuts across class and period of residence. Traditional society generally accepts the class system and accords status through family and social background as well as occupation. Non-traditionalists are most concerned with what people do and a large proportion have links outside the immediate locality. They include the highly mobile manual as well as non-manual workers. Mogey applies a division within the working class, using the terms 'status assent' and 'status dissent' and Klein[4] broadens the concept to one of a state of mind which can occur among either middle or working class. Working-class status assenters are seen by Mogey as those who accept the habits, standards, word usages, and values typical of their area, and to this extent they correspond with Stacey's 'traditionalists'.

Klein sees the attitude towards house ownership as one which differentiates clearly between status assent and dissent, and notes that as researchers have observed an increasing demand for property by members of the working class, dissenters are forming an increasing proportion of this class. She quotes Young and Willmott as saying, 'A house is the bearer of status in any society—it most certainly is in a country where a semi-detached suburban house with a garden has become the signal mark of the middle classes',[5] and observes, 'This is where the ways of assenters and dissenters diverge'.[6]

The proportion of house-owners decreases not only between non-manual and manual workers but also between skilled, semi-skilled,

1. 'Urbanism and suburbanism as ways of life: a re-valuation of definitions.'
2. *Tradition and Change.*
3. *Family and Neighbourhood.*
4. *Samples from English Cultures*, vol. 1.
5. *Family and Kinship in East London.*
6. *Samples from English Cultures*, p. 240.

and unskilled manual workers, and on other evidence such as aspiration for their children and self-ascribed status, it seems likely that the proportion of status assenters in these groups shows an upward trend. The correspondingly higher proportion of dissenters among skilled workers may well be related to their opportunity to realize goals previously largely the prerogative of the middle class. It is probably within this group that there has been the greatest progress towards narrowing the gap between the non-manual salary and the manual wage, and although in many ways other than income—for example, in security of employment, number of hours worked, pension rights—distinctions are still very real ones, when compared with pre-war conditions the gains are clear. Considering only take-home pay, the income of skilled manual workers usually reaches and often exceeds that of such non-manual employees as local government and civil service clerical workers, bank clerks, and junior school teachers. Equal earning opportunity combined with an equal exposure to the pressures of the mass media is likely to result in at least a superficial appearance of equality of status. For example, clothes, car, kitchen equipment, and so on are likely to be indistinguishable to all except the most persistent class identifier. This new phenomenon is doubtless responsible for the often heard statement that class distinctions are disappearing and underlies theories of the 'embourgoisement' of the working class.

Klein sees this economic improvement as an encouragement to the working-class status dissenter, and says:

when social norms have to be created because the old ones are no longer congenial to status dissenters, the mass media will have considerable impact . . . In these circumstances a man is not necessarily driven towards conformity and mass society. He may move towards greater individuation instead.[7]

So in Maghull the manual worker's families living side by side with the non-manual are not likely to feel labelled 'working class' by their possessions. In this respect they are not likely to differ to any great extent from their workmates on the Kirkby estate. Yet there is little doubt that the man who can say he lives in Maghull will be accorded higher status than the one who lives in Kirkby. Each will also hold a position within the separate hierarchies of private or corporation estates.

Bordessa[8] has examined the status accorded to Merseyside areas by residents in three south Liverpool wards, and says: 'Certain districts of a city develop a unique identity giving rise to an overall

7. *Samples from English Cultures*, pp. 276–7.
8. R. Bordessa, *Perception of Social Environment and Residential Desires: A South Liverpool view of the City and Merseyside*, Liverpool Ph.D. thesis, 1971.

image, related to the perceived social status of the district.' By asking respondents to name up to three areas which they most preferred and least preferred he found distinct patterns of preferences and dislikes, unrelated to the class of the respondent. Working-class areas in the inner city and local authority developments outside the city were generally regarded as undesirable and among such areas the most disliked were recent developments. Kirkby was mentioned by half the respondents as a disliked area. He also found the desired pattern of movement by working class (those households where the chief wage-earner was in a manual occupation) to be to 'locationally close but socially distant areas', nearly two-thirds giving preference to middle-class suburbs, while his middle-class city respondents preferred middle-class areas outside the conurbation. He concluded that there is a hierarchy of areas to which people aspire at different stages of life; and that 'the conversion of aspirations to actions is attendant upon economic factors'.

It would appear from this evidence and the evidence from many community studies that areas acquire status as they become established and their reputation is formed through a combination of factors carrying different weights. For private housing estates, these will include the range of house prices, house design and layout, density and proportion of residents in professional and upper managerial occupations. For corporation housing estates, length of construction seems to be the factor most closely related to status, perhaps because the sorting process in which those with least resources have moved away has had more time to operate. On such long-established estates also the age structure is an older one, with fewer teenage children to disturb the peace and lead to friction between neighbours. Another important factor appears to be the proportion of houses to flats and maisonettes. High block flats in particular reflect a low status on their tenants. In all these respects Kirkby must be accounted a low status estate.

Klein suggests that a higher proportion of working-class status dissenters are likely to be found on the new estates than in the old areas, because the assenters will find greater difficulty in adjustment and in facing the economic difficulties of high rents and other new responsibilities, and so are more likely to return home. So again a long-established estate will contain fewer assenters than a new one such as Kirkby. It was suggested in the Kirkby report, however, that some of the less satisfied, likely to move away, might be identified as status dissenters, finding the area 'too working class' and containing people they would prefer not to mix with. The high proportion feeling they had not enough privacy—one-third in all, compared with 12 per cent in Maghull—is probably related to this group.

The distinction between status assenting and dissenting is not a static one, but part of a process of change in which 'dissenting' is gaining ground. Equally so the dissenters are not themselves a homogeneous group, and again as opportunities and aspirations increase new forms of action result. Among working-class dissenters there are those who accept their working-class identity only in the work situation. Zweig[9] provides a number of examples of such men including one who says: 'The class distinctions are at work, but not otherwise.' There are also those of the same occupational group who no longer see themselves as working class, who may perhaps aspire to see their craft accorded professional status and who recognize only the barriers between themselves and those unwilling to make use of their improved material situation to discard the values and traditions of working-class society. While the first may well take the advantages offered by a corporation estate to move further away from the traditional values, the second will reject the estate itself as a working-class institution.

Kirkby and Maghull therefore provide two possible choices to the working-class dissenter, whose constraints may be identical. For other Kirkby residents, constraints may be so great that choice is at a minimum while for other Maghull people constraints are fewer and other choices may follow. Where constraints allow further choice, the decision to remain or move on may depend upon the development of a social system at least at a rudimentary level with which integration is possible. Both Kirkby and Maghull are localities whose evolution is studied here at an early stage and direction of each is still in doubt.

Margaret Stacey, in attempting to justify the study of social relations in localities, sees two aspects of relevance to general sociological theory which may be considered here: first, the establishment and maintenance of a local social system, and second, local conditions in which no such system could be expected.[1] She sees one condition for the development of such a system to be time, preferably a long enough period for the majority of the population to have been born and bred in the locality. In addition, however, common group beliefs and expectations are crucial in its formation.

Neither Kirkby nor Maghull at the time of the surveys can be considered to be 'communities', where the concept of community is defined in such a way as to involve the acknowledgement by its residents, or at least the majority of them, of an emotional attach-

9. F. Zweig, *The Worker in an Affluent Society*, Heinemann, 1961, p. 135.
1. M. Stacey, 'The myth of community studies', *British Journal of Sociology*, xx (1969).

ment to the area such as appears to result largely where a close network of intercommunication occurs at a number of levels.

Nevertheless it would seem that in Kirkby there is a potential for the development of a local social system. Employment is available nearby, and evidence has been provided that it was increasingly being taken up by Kirkby residents, including many wives. This is in contrast to Maghull and so might be expected to provide a source of contacts additional to those common to the two areas. However, while only 5 per cent of Kirkby respondents had met acquaintances at work, over a quarter of Maghull contacts were made in this way. At the same time much the same proportion of contacts in both areas were made simply by being neighbours, and further examination of the frequency and type of contacts made, other than those with relatives, seems to reveal a paradox. Maghull appears to provide a minimum of opportunities for social interaction—there are few clubs or societies or similar facilities—yet many more contacts are made within the estate, outside the immediate vicinity of the home, than between neighbours. In Kirkby, on the other hand, while rather more acquaintances are made on the basis of being neighbours, few contacts are made away from the street in which the home is located.

Maghull in other ways shows wider-ranging communications than does Kirkby, whose residents keep up comparatively few contacts with non-relatives living in their previous home area, unlike a substantial proportion of Maghull people who keep in touch with acquaintances made before their move. It does not appear that this is balanced by a greater contact by Kirkby people with close relatives. Clearly the data provide only quantitative evidence and qualitatively there may be differences unrecognized by the particular inquiries made. But at the level of once-monthly contacts or more, visits to and from parents occurred at much the same frequency within both areas, even though many Maghull parents lived further away than Liverpool, the home of the great majority of Kirkby parents. A marginally greater frequency involved only the parents of Kirkby wives.

Family networks on the two estates appear equally loose-knit, but Maghull residents in retaining a greater number of contacts beyond the boundaries of their locality may have provided themselves with a wider-ranging social network which may compensate them for this in a way not available to many in Kirkby. Taking this into account, and the strong ties with Liverpool which both areas experience through upbringing and economic dependence, as well as facilities for leisure, the development of a local social system in Maghull would appear to be less likely than in Kirkby. Certainly at the time of the survey evidence for such a system there appeared slight. Only perhaps their apparent stability—the small proportion of spiralists and the evident willingness of the majority to see Maghull as their long-term home rather than as a temporary resting place— suggests that a social system will develop in time, but time of a different order from that which, optimistically, may be expected to be needed in Kirkby. Kirkby, with so much less freedom of choice for most residents, either through economic or psychological restraints, and so much dissatisfaction, may be forced by circumstances into a working social system while Maghull remains an area recognizable in geographical rather than social terms. How far this will compensate for a too hastily contrived scheme of development and how nearly Kirkby can approach the satisfaction gained by Maghull residents is another question.

At the present moment at least, there is no evidence to suggest that any corporation housing estate, however much of a 'community', will be more than a 'second best' for the majority of its residents. However disapprovingly the search for status may be regarded by those who have already achieved it, there is little doubt that at least in the foreseeable future, sacrifices—both economic and social— will continue to be made in order to acquire it and the middle-class estate will provide its reward in the fulfilment of aspirations.

Additional tables: Kirkby

TABLE 26

Number of generations in Kirkby households

No. of generations	General sample %	Crown St. sample %
One	10	13
Two	85	85
Three	5	3
No. of households	183	108

TABLE 27

Basis of tenancy of Kirkby households

Basis of tenancy	General sample		Crown St. sample	
	No.	%	No.	%
Housing need	95	52	72	67
Demolition	22	12	16	15
Medical reasons	10	5	4	4
Exchange and transfer	35	19	12	11
De-requisitioning	5	3	1	1
Nominated tenant	3	2	2	2
Other	10	5	—	—
Key worker	3	2	1	
Total	183	100	108	100

TABLE 28

*Number of rooms occupied per household in
Kirkby and the Crown Street area 1961*

No. of rooms occupied	Kirkby survey		Crown St. area 1961*		
	General sample	Crown St. sample	Aber-cromby	Low Hill	Smith-down
	%	%	%	%	%
One	—	—	24	4	1
Two	9	13	19	6	5
Three	23	20	15	8	7
Four	32	39	20	24	51
Five	27	20	8	23	18
Six and over	9	7	13	36	18

* 1961 Census data.

TABLE 29

Size of Kirkby households

No. of persons	General sample		Crown St. sample	
	No.	%	No.	%
One	3	2	9	8
Two	18	10	7	6
Three	20	11	16	15
Four	44	24	16	15
Five	35	19	17	16
Six	29	16	18	17
Seven	19	19	8	7
Over seven	15	8	17	16
Total	183	100	108	100

TABLE 30

Birthplace of Kirkby heads of household and their wives

Birthplace	General sample Head No.	General sample Head %	General sample Wife No.	General sample Wife %	Crown St. sample Head No.	Crown St. sample Head %	Crown St. sample Wife No.	Crown St. sample Wife %
Crown St. districts	8	5	3	2	15	14	15	14
Neighbouring wards	26	14	24	13	24	22	23	21
Other parts of inner Liverpool	70	38	88	48	25	23	23	21
Total inner Liverpool*	104	57	115	63	64	59	61	56
Total outer Liverpool†	24	13	24	13	8	7	10	9
Total Liverpool	128	70	139	76	72	66	71	65
Other parts of Merseyside	12	7	5	3	1	1	6	6
Other parts of U.K.	19	10	14	8	9	8	3	3
N. Ireland	1	1	—	—	1	1	1	1
Eire	—	—	—	—	6	6	2	2
Elsewhere	2	1	14	7	3	3	1	1
Not known	21	11	11	6	16	15	24	22
Total all groups	183	100	183	100	108	100	108	100

* 1951 Census sub-divisions ɪa, ɪɪa, ɪɪb.
† 1951 Census sub-divisions ɪɪc, ɪɪɪa, ɪɪɪb.

TABLE 31

Birthplace of Kirkby wives related to that of their husbands

Birthplace of head of household	Birthplace of wife	General sample %	Crown St. sample %
Inner Liverpool*	Inner Liverpool	46	45
	Outer Liverpool	5	5
	Elsewhere	3	5
Outer Liverpool†	Inner Liverpool	7	4
	Outer Liverpool	4	3
	Elsewhere	2	—
Merseyside excluding Liverpool	Inner Liverpool	4	1
	Outer Liverpool	1	—
	Elsewhere	1	—
Elsewhere	Inner Liverpool	6	8
	Outer Liverpool	1	2
	Elsewhere	4	2
Not known		16	25

* 1951 Census sub-divisions ɪa, ɪɪa, ɪɪb. ɪɪɪa, ɪɪɪb.
† 1951 Census sub-divisions ɪɪc,

TABLE 32

Time lived in Liverpool by Kirkby heads of
household and their wives

Time lived in Liverpool	General sample				Crown St. sample			
	Head		Wife		Head		Wife	
	No.	%	No.	%	No.	%	No.	%
Always	155	85	159	87	77	71	76	70
Fifteen years or more	9	5	6	3	10	9	6	6
Less than fifteen years	15	8	10	5	6	6	4	4
Not known, not applicable	4	2	8	4	15	14	22	20
Total	183	100	183	100	108	100	108	100

TABLE 33

Type of accommodation occupied by Kirkby
households at previous and present place of residence

Type of accommodation	General sample		Crown St. sample	
	Previous	Present	Previous	Present
	%	%	%	%
House, let unfurnished	43	62	26	42
House, let furnished	6	—	—	—
Private flat, unfurnished	8	—	8	—
Private flat, furnished	1	—	4	—
Corporation flat: block	—	20	—	30
maisonette	—	5	—	13
other	6	11	5	15
Rooms, unfurnished*	27	—	35	—
Rooms, furnished	8	—	16	—
Other†	1	—	—	—
Not known	—	1	6	—

* Including living with parents.   † Including prefabs, caravans.

TABLE 34

*Rents paid by Kirkby households in 1960 and
Crown Street area households in 1956*

Rent	Kirkby survey (1960)				Crown St. (1956)	
	General sample		Crown St. sample			
	No.	%	No.	%	No.	%
Under 15s.	4	2	7	6	282	53
15s. to under 25s.	76	42	45	42	163	30
25s. to under 35s.	92	50	50	46	49	9
35s. to under 45s.	8	4	5	5	} 28	} 5
45s. and over	2	1	1	1		
No information, not applicable	1	1	—	—	17	3
Total	183	100	108	100	539	100

TABLE 35

Year of arrival of Kirkby households

Year of arrival	General sample			Crown St. sample		
	South-dene	West-vale	North-wood	South-dene	West-vale	North-wood
	No.	No.	No.	No.	No.	No.
Before 1952	—	—	—	—	—	—
1952	1	—	—	—	—	—
1953	12	—	—	8	—	—
1954	22	—	—	11	—	—
1955	19	3	5	10	2	4
1956	2	20	3	2	8	2
1957	7	19	8	7	10	3
1958	4	5	27	3	3	16
1959	6	—	16	3	—	16
1960	—	—	4	—	—	—
Total	73	47	63	44	23	41

TABLE 36

Kirkby: journey to work, 1961, 1966

Workplace (col. 1), residence (col. 2)	(1) Kirkby residents working elsewhere				(2) Working in Kirkby residence elsewhere			
	1961		1966		1961		1966	
	Men	*Women*	*Men*	*Women*	*Men*	*Women*	*Men*	*Women*
	%	%	%	%	%	%	%	%
Liverpool	78	90	73	88	63	64	55	48
Bootle	8	2	10	2	3	1	3	2
West Lancashire R.D.	3	4	4	6	8	4	7	5
Huyton	6	3	9	3	11	21	10	14
Whiston					2	3	6	11
Other Lancashire	2	—	2	—	8	7	16	18
Birkenhead	—	—	—	—	—	—	—	—
Wallasey	2	—	1	—	2	—	1	1
Other Cheshire	—	—	—	—	1	—	1	1
Other England and Wales	1	—	1	1	1	—	1	—
Total number	7,000	2,700	7,350	3,270	9,200	4,000	11,500	3,900
Percentage of all occupied residents	54	45	56	36	—	—	—	—

Source: 1961, 1966 (10 per cent sample) Censuses.

TABLE 37

Social classification of occupations

Occupation	Social class
Non-manual:	
Administrative, professional and managerial	I and II
Shopkeepers and other small employers	
Clerical workers	
Shop assistants	III
Personal service (including domestics, barmen, waitresses)	
Manual:	
Foremen	III
Skilled workers	
Semi-skilled workers	IV
Unskilled workers	V

TABLE 38

Change of work by heads of household on move to Kirkby

Change	General sample		Crown St. sample	
	No.	%	No.	%
To same social class	32	52	24	56
To higher* social class	10	16	6	14
To lower* social class	14	23	—	—
Previously unemployed	1	—	10	23
Now unemployed	—	} 9	1	} 7
Now retired or housewife	4		2	
Total	61	100	43	100
Percentage of total households		33		40

* Level of social class is taken to be reasonably indicated by a scale in which social class I is the 'highest' social class, and social class V the 'lowest'. Non-manual social class III is 'higher' than manual social class III.

TABLE 39

*Cost of journey to work made by Kirkby heads of
household by public transport, 1960*

Cost per day	General sample %	Crown St. sample %
Less than 6d.	2	2
6d. to less than 1s.	13	14
1s. to less than 1s. 6d.	17	9
1s. 6d. to less than 2s.	44	33
2s. to less than 2s. 6d.	9	12
2s. 6d. to less than 3s.	11	16
3s. and over	3	14

TABLE 40

*Means of journey to work made by Kirkby survey heads
of household, 1960 and employed persons, 1966*

Means of journey to work	Kirkby survey General sample %	Kirkby survey Crown St. sample %	Kirkby 1966 Census %
Cycle	10	8	3
Moped	5	1	} 2
Motor-cycle	5	3	
Own car	9	4	} 13
Lift in other's car	1	3	
Public transport	51	63	59
Works bus	6	—	2
Walk	10	13	} 21
No information, other	3	5	
Not applicable (% of all heads of household)	12	31	—

Source: Kirkby survey and 1966 (10 per cent sample) Census.

TABLE 41

Preference for Kirkby over previous place of residence

Reasons given	General sample n = 220 % of items	Crown St. sample n = 139 % of items
Cleaner, fresher, healthier	54	58
More spacious	14	15
Improved accommodation	22	7
Rural surroundings	2	1
Friendliness of residents	1	3
No traffic problems	1	3
Other	2	11
No reason given	3	1

Note. More than one reason may be given by each respondent.

TABLE 42

Preference for previous place of residence over Kirkby

Reasons given	General sample n = 217 % of items	Crown St. sample n = 126 % of items
Convenience for shops	30	31
Neighbourliness	17	23
Convenience for entertainment	10	12
Cheaper living	6	12
Relations nearer	8	1
Always lived there	3	6
More social organizations (including churches)	4	—
Life in general	3	2
Other reasons	8	2
No reason given, no answer	10	11
	% of households	% of households
No preference	33	37

Note. More than one reason may be given by each respondent.

TABLE 43

Reasons given for liking Kirkby accommodation

Reasons given	General sample n = 212 % of items	Crown St. sample n = 128 % of items
Bathroom	11	10
Kitchen	7	5
Space and size	5	7
'Place of own'	6	8
Construction and design	1	3
Generally favourable	48	39
Other	—	1
No answer	19	18
No likes	2	8

Note. More than one reason may be given by each respondent.

TABLE 44

Reasons given for disliking Kirkby accommodation

Reasons given	General sample n = 219 % of items	Crown St. sample n = 129 % of items
Size, number, and design of rooms	26	17
Construction, i.e. workmanship and materials	6	5
Design of chimney, heating arrangements	5	6
Noise, internal or external	10	13
Siting	4	2
Design, other	6	4
Rent	1	3
Other	9	25
No answer	7	9
No specific reasons or no dislikes	26	16

Note. More than one reason may be given by each respondent.

TABLE 45

Home address of Kirkby relatives

Relatives living in	% of all parents		% of all siblings		% of children living away from home
	Head	Wife	Head	Wife	
Kirkby					
General sample	7	6	12	16	10
Crown St. sample	7	7	12	14	23
Inner Liverpool					
General sample	31	45	29	32	36
Crown St. sample	23	37	29	30	48
Outer Liverpool					
General sample	11	7	20	18	20
Crown St. sample	26	15	24	22	6
Elsewhere					
General sample	14	7	33	23	34
Crown St. sample	14	11	31	28	23
Not living or none					
General sample	38	35	6	11	—
Crown St. sample	30	30	4	6	—

TABLE 46

Visits made once a month or more by or to relatives of Kirkby residents

Relatives living in	% of all parents				% of all siblings				% of children living away from home	
	Head		Wife		Head		Wife			
	Visit	Do not visit	Visit	Do not visit	Visit	Do not visit	Visit	Do not visit	Visit	Do not visit
Kirkby										
General sample	7	—	6	—	9	3	13	3	10	—
Crown St. sample	6	1	7	—	8	4	11	3	23	—
Inner Liverpool										
General sample	25	6	39	6	17	12	23	9	34	2
Crown St. sample	17	6	34	3	16	13	20	10	40	8
Outer Liverpool										
General sample	6	5	4	3	14	6	7	11	15	5
Crown St. sample	22	4	13	2	16	8	14	8	6	—
Elsewhere										
General sample	5	9	2	5	27	6	8	15	12	22
Crown St. sample	7	7	7	4	7	24	10	18	9	14

Note. 'Not living or none' category has been omitted.

TABLE 47

Seeing relatives in Kirkby compared with previous residence

Frequency of seeing relatives	General sample		Crown St. sample	
	No.	%	No.	%
Seeing more of relatives in Kirkby	25	14	13	12
Seeing less of relatives in Kirkby	120	65	62	57
Seeing relatives as much in Kirkby	36	20	28	26
No answer, not applicable	2	1	5	5
Total	183	100	108	100

TABLE 48

Home activities in Kirkby compared with previous residence

Home activity	General sample		Crown St. sample	
	Spending more time	Spending less time	Spending more time	Spending less time
	%	%	%	%
Decorating	53	37	63	27
'Do-it-yourself'	33	37	31	37
General family activities	53	31	47	33

Note. Remainder expressed no opinion.

TABLE 49

Attitude to neighbours in Kirkby and previous residence

Attitude	General sample %	Crown St. sample %
(1) 'Getting on all right' with neighbours:		
Do get on	88	84
Do not get on	4	7
Qualified, indifferent, or no answer	8	8
(2) 'Having more to do' with neighbours than previously:		
Have more to do	37	42
Have less to do	35	29
About the same or no answer	28	30
(3) Thinking Kirkby as friendly a place as the previous residence:		
More friendly a place	30	28
Less friendly a place	28	25
As friendly a place	33	36
Don't know or no answer	9	11

TABLE 50

Present and past attendance at entertainments
(by at least one member of the household)

Entertainment	General sample		Crown St. sample	
	Past attendance %	Present %	Past attendance %	Present %
Attending once a week or more than once a week:				
Sports (watching or participating)	37	29	30	28
Pub	48	34	41	26
Cinema	57	11	66	14
Dance	9	7	8	8
Attending less than once a week to once a month:				
Sports	15	17	11	11
Pub	9	13	9	16
Cinema	8	9	6	2
Dance	3	6	—	5
Attending less than once a month or not at all	36	54	34	56

TABLE 51

Location of entertainments attended at present
(by at least one member of the household)

Location	General sample %	Crown St. sample %
All outside Kirkby	34	31
Inside and outside Kirkby	33	38
All inside Kirkby	33	31

Additional tables: Maghull

TABLE 52

Composition of families in the sample

Family composition	%
Nuclear families, with or without children	85
Incomplete nuclear families, widowed/single	10
Extended families, one or more additional relatives in residence	6

TABLE 53

Size of families in the sample

No. of people in family	%
1	7
2	14
3	22
4	39
5	13
6	4
6+	1

Note. The mean family size was 3·5 members per family.

TABLE 54

Reason why respondent moved to Maghull

Reason given	%
Liked the house	36
Employment reasons	22
Liked the area	27
To be near relations	6
Already lived there	3
Retirement	2
No reason given	3
Other reason	1

TABLE 55

Respondent's home before moving to Maghull

Previous home	%
Bootle/Litherland	14
Liverpool	44
Lancashire/Cheshire	28
Elsewhere	14

TABLE 56

Reason for wishing to move from Maghull

Reason given	%
Employment reasons	5
Wanted a better house	5
Wanted to be near relative/friend	4
Other reasons	14
No wish to move	72

TABLE 57

Definite plans for moving from Maghull

Plans for moving	%
Respondents with definite plans	5
Respondents without definite plans	95

TABLE 58

*Place where respondent and spouse (where relevant)
lived in youth*

Place lived in youth	Males %	Females %
Bootle/Litherland	14	15
Liverpool	49	45
Lancashire/Cheshire	21	23
Elsewhere	16	17

TABLE 59

Workplace of head of household

Workplace	%
Maghull/Lydiate	10
Kirkby	10
Aintree/Netherton	9
Liverpool	51
Bootle	5
Lancashire/Cheshire	4
Mobile occupation	5
Not applicable	7

TABLE 60

Age of head of household

Age	%
20–29	5
30–39	36
40–49	30
50–64	22
65 and over	7

TABLE 61

Television ownership

Ownership	%
Households with television	95
Households without television	5

TABLE 62

*Frequency of television viewing in households
with television*

Frequency	%
Every day	73
Less frequently	27

TABLE 63

Television channel watched on night prior to interview in households with television

Channel	%
BBC I exclusively	18
BBC 2 exclusively	4
ITV exclusively	22
Combination of channels	25
Didn't watch	31

TABLE 64

Frequency of visiting public house by head of household and spouse

Frequency	Males %	Females %
At least once a week	47	17
At least once a month	10	14
Less frequently	11	22
Never go	25	43
Not applicable	7	4

TABLE 65

Frequency of visiting cinema

Frequency	%
At least once a week	18
At least once a month	20
Less frequently	42
Never go	21

TABLE 66

Frequency of going to bingo (wives and single women heads of household)

Frequency	%
At least once a week	4
At least once a month	3
Less frequently	7
Never go	86

TABLE 67

Heads of household and regular football support

Regularity of support	%
Watched Liverpool regularly	20
Watched Everton regularly	11
Watched both Liverpool and Everton regularly	2
Watched some other club regularly	2
Do not watch football regularly	65

TABLE 68

Participation in social life of a church (head of household and spouse)

Participation	Males	Females
Took part in church social life	7	16
Didn't take part in church social life	93	84

TABLE 69

Frequency of social interaction of household with people other than relatives

Frequency of interaction	%
At least once a week	50
At least once a month	32
Less frequently	18

TABLE 70

*Contacts according to which member of respondent's
family interacted*

Interaction by	%
Husband alone	8
Wife alone	32
Husband and wife together	60

Note. Tables 71–3 are concerned with social interaction with people other than relatives of the household head and his wife and are compiled from 428 contacts reported by the respondents in reply to the question 'Do you visit anyone in their home, or they you?'

TABLE 71

Contacts according to where contact lived

Home of contact	%
In same street	25
Elsewhere in Maghull	35
Respondent's home town	14
Elsewhere	26

TABLE 72

*Contacts according to how the respondent
met the contact*

How contact made	%
At pre-Maghull residence	21
At work	28
Through being neighbours	31
Through group membership	11
In some other way	9

TABLE 73

Privacy

Feelings about privacy	%
Enough	87
Not enough	12
No view	1

TABLE 74

Social life

Feelings about own social life	%
Good	6
Adequate	32
Poor	52
No new	9

TABLE 75

Attitudes towards the provision of services in Maghull

Respondent's attitude towards	Good %	Adequate %	Poor %	No view %
Shopping provision	57	37	6	—
Public transport	39	41	13	8
Primary school provision	65	12	1	23
Secondary school provision	43	17	2	38
Leisure facilities for schoolchildren	11	31	34	25
Leisure facilities for adolescents	5	20	51	25
Provision of entertainment	1	17	77	5
Hospital services	34	40	20	6
Provision of clinics	49	22	2	27
Old people's welfare	32	21	10	37

APPENDIX C

Notes on sampling methods

The selection of the Kirkby sample has been described in Chapter 2 and of the Maghull sample in Chapter 9.

All the addresses selected in Kirkby except four in the General sample and one in the Crown Street sample contained only one family; these five each contained two. In corporation estates, formal sharing of accommodation is not allowed and it has, therefore, been assumed that all those living at an address, whatever their relationship to the head, form a single household by Census definition.

Under these circumstances, estimates of sampling errors in the Kirkby sample may be based on those appropriate to a simple random sample, to which the systematic sample used here closely approximates.

The sampling error of a proportion derived from such a sample may be expressed:

$$S.E._p = \sqrt{\left[\frac{p(1-p)}{N}\right]}$$

x_j is the number of units corresponding to p in that sample where p is the sample proportion and N is the number of units in the sample.

It may then be stated with 95 per cent confidence that the proportion in the population from which the sample has been drawn lies between $p \pm 1.96\ S.E._p$.

In the Maghull report percentages given for the whole survey area have been weighted in order to compensate for the different sampling fractions[1] used in the six sub-areas and

$$p = \sum_1^6 \frac{w_i x_i}{N}$$

where p is the proportion in the total sample, x_i is the number of units corresponding to p in that sample, w_i is the reciprocal of the sampling fraction in the ith sub-area, n_i is the number of units in the ith sub-area sample and $N = \sum_1^6 w_i n_i$.

1. See p. 84.

The maximum standard error of p is then:[2]

$$S.E._p = \frac{1}{N}\sqrt{\left[\sum_1^6 \frac{w_i^2 n_i}{4} - \frac{(p - \frac{1}{2})^2}{\sum_1^6 n_i}\right]}.$$

2. See E. Gittus in Appendix B of *Technical Change and Industrial Relations,* Liverpool University Press, 1956.

The Halewood estate

It is of interest to compare the situation in Kirkby with that in another large Liverpool housing estate, Halewood, constructed five years later just outside the city boundary. Some differences between the two estates may indicate factors of significance in determining the attitudes of residents to their new situation.

The Halewood survey was carried out in 1966 at the request of the Liverpool Personal Service Society who were concerned with some difficulties of adjustment which they had met on the estate. Households were interviewed, selected by means of a 1 in 10 sample of addresses taken from the electoral register. A total of 336 interviews were made, a response rate of 92 per cent.

By 1960 when the first Halewood families moved into the estate, although there were still very many families on Liverpool's housing list in need of accommodation, an even more urgent problem was to house those displaced by demolition in the areas where redevelopment was at last under way in earnest. Differences in age structure and household composition between Kirkby and Halewood therefore reflect a changing emphasis in the city's housing policy. Although Halewood residents had, like Kirkby's, largely been moved from central areas of the city, they had not generally been living in such overcrowded conditions. The majority had moved from houses rather than shared accommodation, and there were even a few previous owner-occupiers. The proportion of manual workers was very similar to that in Kirkby, though there was a slightly higher proportion with skilled and semi-skilled occupations.

The Halewood estate itself shows rather more variety in housing layout than Kirkby, although it is similarly set in a rather bleak area of countryside with little attempt at landscaping. Only three high blocks of flats had been built at the time of the survey, but there were proportionately more maisonettes and four-storey flats than in Kirkby. In one of its three neighbourhoods, Mackets Lane, a large proportion of the houses are semi-detached or terrace, often with their own garages and integrating closely with the adjacent privately owned houses, while the remaining accommodation of two-storey flats and maisonettes differ little in appearance from the houses. Here there are a number of local shops available and the amenities, appearance and general air of prosperity resemble closely those of most suburban private housing estates.

Because the Halewood tenants had largely been moved from re-development areas of old housing, their age structure showed a wider range than that in Kirkby, including a higher proportion in the 40 and upward age groups (Table 76a). The child population consequently, though still high by city standards, was lower than that of Kirkby, with quite a substantial number between 15 and 20 years old (Table 76b), most of whom had left school and were in

TABLE 76

Age structure of Halewood survey residents

(a) Heads of household

Age group	%
20–29	10
30–39	26
40–49	24
50–59	18
60–64	5
65 and over	11
Not known	6
No. of households	336

(b) All residents

Age group	%
0–4	16
5–14	24
15–20	15
21–59	37
60 and over	8
No. of individuals in survey households	1,511

employment. As a result, in half the Halewood households there was more than one wage-earner, and as many as 20 per cent had three or more. The easier circumstances of many families on the estate is reflected in car ownership. One-quarter of the respondents owned cars, compared with about 10 per cent[1] in Kirkby at the time of the survey.

Although the majority of Halewood tenants had not applied for a corporation tenancy, and might therefore be expected to be more critical of their new house or flat, only 7 per cent compared with Kirkby's 21 per cent wanted to change their accommodation, and no more than in Kirkby—about one-third of households—said that they wanted to move out of the estate entirely. Most significant was that in Mackets Lane, where housing is most similar to that of private estates, in spite of very high rents there was a significantly higher level of satisfaction than in the other two neighbourhoods.

1. The question from which this figure is obtained asked for the means of travel to work. Nine per cent used their own car, and it is assumed that nearly all of those owning a car would use it for this purpose.

Many tenants here have moved in by exchange or transfer: they have been able to exercise choice.

For the remainder and majority of residents there had probably been less choice in their move to the estate than for Kirkby tenants, in that in many cases they had been forced by redevelopment to make the move rather than by housing need. Nevertheless there was no more dissatisfaction than in Kirkby, and in some respects less. Life cycle stage is the most obvious difference between the two estates, associated with greater prosperity for the older households with a number of wage-earners. A second factor is greater use of local employment particularly by the women, many of whom worked at a large car factory nearby. It is tempting to suggest that Halewood's economic advantages have resulted in a rather better social climate than in Kirkby.

The Kirkby questionnaire

UNIVERSITY OF
LIVERPOOL

INFORMATION ABOUT EACH MEMBER OF THE HOUSEHOLD

Name of informant

DEPARTMENT OF
SOCIAL SCIENCE

SOCIAL
ADJUSTMENT
AT KIRKBY

Address:

Neighbourhood:

Code number:

Date of
interview:

Initials of
interviewer:

(In administering,
substitute for the
expression 'Crown Street'
the name of the street
in that district in which
respondent last resided)

	1	*2*	*3*	*4*	*5*	*6*	*7*	*a*	*8*	*9*
	Personal name	*Reln. to*	*Mar. stat.*	*Date of birth*	*Town of birth*	*Full address (if Liverpool)*	*Occupation*	*Full?*	*Firm (or school)*	*Location*
1.	Head of h/h									
2.										
3.										
4.										
5.										
6.										
7.										
8.										

10. Is there anyone else who belongs to this household, but who is at present away from home (e.g. in the forces, at sea, or in hospital)? If so, record details above.

II PROPERTY LAST OCCUPIED IN CROWN STREET DISTRICT

11.   Address

12.   Number of households in that dwelling

13. a.   Type of accommodation: house/flat/tenement/room(s)
    b.   Was that accommodation let: furnished/unfurnished

14. a.   Was there any member of the household at the 'Crown Street' address who is not a member of the household here at Kirkby?
                                                         Yes/No
    b.   If yes, please give:

Personal name	Surname	Reln. to head of present household	Date of birth	Present address
(i)				As Q. 11 above/
(ii)				As Q. 11 above/
(iii)				As Q. 11 above/
(iv)				As Q. 11 above/

15. a.   Are there any members of the *present* household who were not living at the 'Crown Street' address?   Yes/No
    b.   If yes, give ref. number(s) from page 1

III EMPLOYMENT

(Ask all questions in this section of *main* wage-earner, No.   )

16. a.   When you (he) came to live at Kirkby, had you (he) the same job as your (his) present one?   Same/Different
    b.   If 'different', give:
         Occupation   Firm   Location   Reason for change

17.   Did you come to Kirkby to be nearer to your work?   Yes/No

18. a.   How do you travel to work?
         Walk   Motor-cycle   Public transport
         Cycle   Own car   Works transport
         Moped   Lift in car
         If public transport:
    b.   How much per day is the cost?

IV RESIDENTIAL CHANGE

If not born in Liverpool

19. a. When did you first come to Liverpool?   (i) Man
    b.   (ii) Wife

20. a. Did you want to come and live at Kirkby?   Yes/No
    b. If yes, why?
       If no, why did you come?

21. a. Do you wish to move away from this house/flat?   Yes/No
    b. Why?
    c. Do other members of your family wish to move away from this
       house/flat?   Yes/No
    d. Why?
    e. Which members of your family are you referring to?
                                                   Spouse/Other (state)
    If response to Q. 21a above is yes:

22. a. Would you prefer to move away from Kirkby, or to remain
       (assuming that you could get suitable accommodation wherever
       you chose to go)?   Move/Remain
    b. Why?
    c. If you wish to move away from Kirkby, where would you wish
       to go?
    d. Why?
    e. If you wish to remain in Kirkby, where would you wish to go?
    f. Why?

V KINSHIP AND FAMILY

		How often do	
		You visit	*They visit*
23.	Where do (*or did*) the following live?	*them*	*you*
	a. Parents of head of the household		
	b. Parents of his wife		
	c. Brothers of the head		
	d. Sisters of the head		
	e. Brothers of the wife		
	f. Sisters of the wife		
	g. Sons of the head not living at this address		
	h. Daughters of the head not living at this address		

24.   Record above, alongside relevant persons, frequency of visits.

25. a. Do you see your relatives about as often as when you were living in 'Crown Street', or more of them, or less of them?

Same/More/Less

   b. If 'More', or 'less', why?

26.   Do you rely more on your relatives, or less on them, since you came to Kirkby, or would you say there is little difference?

More/Less/Little difference (+comment)

27. a. If you were ill and needed looking after, who would now do this for you?

   b. Who would look after your housework and children?

28. a. If, when you were living in 'Crown Street, you had been ill and needed looking after, who would have done this for you then?

   b. And who would have looked after your housework and children?

29.   Have you bought any new articles for the home because you came to live in Kirkby (such as furniture, soft furnishings, floor coverings, carpet, washing machine, vacuum cleaner, TV, radio, etc.)?

30.   Are you buying anything *now* on hire purchase?   Yes/No

31.   If yes, what are you buying?   *How much per week?*

   (i)

   (ii)

   (iii)

      (checks, clubs)

32.   Have you bought any articles second hand?

(Ask about male householder only)   *Whether done by husband and wife together*

33.   Do you spend any time gardening?   Yes/No

   a. If yes, how much?   Summer   Yes/No (b)

   c.   Winter   Yes/No (d)

34. a. Have *you* done any decorating in your home in the past two years?

Yes/No

   b. If yes, what have you done   Yes/No (c)

   d. Is this more than you used to do at 'Crown Street'?   Yes/No

35. a. Do you make things for the home?   Yes/No

   b. If yes, what things?   Yes/No (c)

   d. Is this more than you did at 'Crown Street'?   Yes/No

36. a. Have you a TV set?   Yes/No

   b. If yes, how often do you view?   Every day/Less often (c)

   d. If 'less often', specify:

   e. Do you now view more often than you did at 'Crown Street'?

Yes/No

37.   Do you think that nowadays the activities you do together as a family take up more of your time than when you were living at 'Crown Street'?   Yes/No (+any comment).

38.   Where do you do most of your shopping for:
    a. Groceries?   c. Clothing?
    b. Greengroceries?   d. Furniture?
    Only to be asked of parents whose children went to school in 'Crown Street' and Kirkby

39.   Where did your children go to school in 'Crown Street'?

                    Personal name   *School(s)*
        (i)
        (ii)
        (iii)
        (iv)

40.   Do you prefer 'Crown Street' schools or Kirkby schools, for:
    a. (i) Buildings?   'C.S.'/Kirkby. Why?   (b)
    c. (ii) Teaching?   'C.S.'/Kirkby. Why?   (d)
    e. (iii) Meals?   'C.S.'/Kirkby. Why?   (f)
    g. (iv) Recreation? 'C.S.'/Kirkby. Why?   (h)

VI INFORMAL INTERACTION

(*Informant only*) Who do you know at Kirkby, other than relatives, starting from your next-door neighbours? For example:

		Location			Frequency	How got to know
		Next door	2/3 doors away	Further (give road)		
41.	Do you visit anyone in their homes, or they you?	. . .	. . .	. . .	. . .	. . .
42.	Do you go out with anyone else, e.g.	. . .	. . .	. . .	. . .	. . .
	a. Shopping?	. . .	. . .	. . .	. . .	. . .
	b. Cinema?	. . .	. . .	. . .	. . .	. . .
	c. Public house?	. . .	. . .	. . .	. . .	. . .
	d. Club?	. . .	. . .	. . .	. . .	. . .
	e. Other reasons (state)?	. . .	. . .	. . .	. . .	. . .

Use separate line for each contact.

If the same person appears in more than one category, please underline second and subsequent entries, in Location columns.

Entries in the first two Location columns ('next door' and '2/3 doors away') may be indicated by means of ticks.

Frequency-code: W = at least once a week; M = less than once a week but at least once a month; L = less than once a month.

Code for 'How got to know':

1 = from pre-Kirkby place of residence.
2 = through work contact, self or spouse.
3 = through common group membership—religious based.
5 = meeting during shopping in Kirkby.
6 = meeting when taking children to school or fetching them.
7 = at clinic.

Neighbours: thinking of these as people living near you:

43. a. Would you say you got on all right with your neighbours?
Yes/No (+any comment)

   b. Would you prefer your 'Crown Street' neighbours?
Yes/No (+any comment)

   c. Do your children and those of your neighbours play together?
Yes/No (+any comment)

   d. Do you have more to do with your neighbours here in Kirkby than
with your 'Crown Street' neighbours when you were living there,
or less to do with them, or about the same?
More/Less/about the same (+any comment)

44. a. Do any of your neighbours borrow from you?   Yes/No

   b. If need arises do they lend to you?   Yes/No

45.   Do you think that Kirkby is as friendly a place as 'Crown Street',
or more friendly, or less friendly?
As friendly/More/Less (+any comment)

46.   Thinking of your friends as people who are not relatives whom you
know quite well, do most of your friends live in Kirkby, or are they
living in or near 'Crown Street', or are they scattered about?
Kirkby/Crown Street/Scattered

47. a. Do you visit friends or old neighbours in or near 'Crown Street'?
Yes/No

   b. If yes, how often?

VII VOLUNTARY ASSOCIATIONS

48. a. Do any members of your household belong to or attend associations
such as the Mothers' Union, Catholic Mothers' Meeting, housewives' clubs: working men's clubs, ex-service clubs such as R.A.F.A.,
political groups, tenants' or ratepayers' associations; works clubs;
trade unions; or O.A.P. club. If they do, record below. (*Start with
church services*)

Personal name	*Name of association or club*	*Location*	*Frequency of attendance*
	(Church services)		
	(Sunday school)		
	(Works club)		
	(Trade union)		

   b. And similarly when you were living at 'Crown Street'?
If so, note below:

	(Church services)		
	(Sunday school)		
	(Works club)		
	(Trade union)		

    c. Do any of your children under the age of 18 attend any youth clubs and/or associations such as boys' or girls' clubs, guides, Boys'
    d. Brigade, Church Lads' Brigade, or Life Boys?. If they do, record above. (*Start with Sunday school*). Then record similarly in relation to 'Crown Street'.

49. a. Is there any kind of club, group or other association which you think Kirkby should have?   Yes/No

    b. If yes, state what:

        (49. c.) *Would you (your family) go to it?*

        (i)   Yes/No

        (ii)   Yes/No

        (iii)   Yes/No

50.   Have you been visited by any church representative in the past month?   Yes/No

51.   If not attending church now, but attending when at 'Crown Street'

    a. Are there any particular reasons why you do not go to church at Kirkby?   Man: Yes/No.   Wife: Yes/No

      If yes, what are they?   Man: Wife:

    b. Do you feel that you belong to any particular denomination?
                                  Man: Yes/No.   Wife: Yes/No

    c. If yes, state which: Man: Wife:

52. a. (*Of all*) Do you think that people are being brought together by the churches in Kirkby?   Man: Yes/No.   Wife: Yes/No

    b. Why do you say this?   Man: Wife:

VIII ENTERTAINMENT

53.   Do any members of your household (a) watch sports, e.g. football, cricket (b) play sports (c) go to a public house (d) go to the cinema (e) go to dances? If so, note below:

Personal name	Activity	Location	Frequency

54.   And similarly, when you were living at 'Crown Street'? If so, note below (a) to (e).

IX COMMUNITY ORIENTATIONS

55. If you think of 'Crown Street' and then of Kirkby:
    a. In what ways is Kirkby to be preferred?
    b. In what ways is 'Crown Street' to be preferred?

56. a. (*Ask housewife*) Do you feel lonely living at Kirkby?   Yes/No
    b. Why?

57. a. What do you like about your house (flat)?
    b. What do you dislike about it?

58. Do you think you have enough privacy?
                                          Yes/No (+any comment)

59. What do you think of the way Kirkby has been planned and designed?

60. What do you think of the facilities at Kirkby for:
    a. Shopping   e. Social life
    b. Public transport   f. Entertainment
    c. Schoolchildren (leisure)   d. Hospital treatment
    d. Young people (juveniles)   h. Clinics
              i. Old People's Welfare

61. In most places there are people who take the lead in matters of importance to local residents:
    a. Who do you think of as doing this at Kirkby?
    b. What is your opinion of leadership at Kirkby?

62. Would you prefer leaders to come from people connected with:
    (i) Politics   Yes/No
    (ii) The churches   Yes/No
    (iii) Trade unions   Yes/No
    (iv) Anything else (state what)   Yes/No

63. a. Are there some kinds of people in Kirkby you prefer not to mix with?   Yes/No
    b. If yes, what sort of people

64. If someone remarked that Kirkby was not such a good class area as some of the newer parts of the Liverpool area, would you agree or disagree?   Agree/Disagree (+any comment)

65. Do you feel satisfied with the way the Kirkby U.D.C. is managing with local problems?   Yes/No (+any comment)

The Maghull questionnaire

Maghuʾl questionnaire

Code No: Address: Type of house: Date of Interview:

Name of each member of each household	Relationship to	Date of birth	Marital status	Occupation	Firm/school	Place of work
1	Head of household					
2						
3						
4						
5						
6						
7						
8						
9						
10						

N.B. Retired/Unemployed; state previous occupation also. Housewife may have part-time occupation.

RESIDENCE

If the answer is Liverpool say which part

In which town did you live in your youth?

In which town did your husband/wife live?

Where did you live before coming to Maghull?

How long have you been living in Maghull?   years

Why did you choose the Maghull area to live in?

Why did you move from your previous residence?

Did you consider moving to any other area?   Yes/No

If yes, which area?

Do you wish to move away from Maghull?   Yes/No

If yes, where would you like to go?

If yes, why do you wish to move away?

Do you have any definite plans for moving?

What was the occupation of:

    The husband's father

    The wife's father

FAMILY AND KINSHIP (1)

Where do (or did) the following people live?	*How often do you visit them?*	*How often do they visit you?*
Husband's parents		
Wife's parents		
Brothers of husband		
Sisters of husband		
Brothers of wife		
Sisters of wife		

Fill in right-hand column as follows: D Daily; W At least once a week; M At least once a month; O Less than once a month.

FAMILY AND KINSHIP (2)

If the wife were ill and needed
looking after, who would do this?

                                       Husband   *Wife*

How many nights were spent at
home with the family last week?

Do you have a television set?   Yes/No

What programmes did you watch last night? (*As many as possible. Indicate which channel*)

How often do you view?   Every day/Less often

RECREATION

When did you last go to the cinema?
Where did you go? (Name/Town)
Where do you usually go?
When did the husband last go to the pub?
Where did he go? (Name/Town)
Where does he usually go?
When did the wife last go to a pub?
Where did she go? (Name/Town)
Where does she usually go?
When did you last go to a club?
Where did you go? (Name/Town)
Where do you usually go?
When did you last go to a theatre?
Where did you go (Name/Town)
When did the husband last go to a football match?
Is he a regular football watcher?   Yes/No
Which team does he support?
When did the wife last go to Bingo?
Where did she go? (Town/Name)
What other recreational activities do you take part in, outside the home?

Informal interaction (other than family)	Who visits or is visited?	Is the person from:				Frequency of visit	How did you get to know them?	Do you also go:					Specify other:
		Same street	Maghull	Home town	Elsewhere			Shopping	Cinema	Pub	Club	Other places	
Do you visit anyone in their home, or does anyone visit you? 1													
2													
3													
4													
5													
6													
7													
8													
Do you go out with anyone else? Shopping													
To a cinema													
To a pub													
On any other occasion													

SHOPPING

Where do you, or your wife go, on the following days for the following articles? (*Ring the appropriate numbers*)

	Local shops	Central Square	Central Liverpool	Elsewhere
Monday to Friday	I	2	4	8
Saturday	I	2	4	8
Groceries	I	2	4	8
Clothes	I	2	4	8
Furniture	I	2	4	8

If elsewhere please specify the place.

Monday to Friday

Saturday   Clothes

Groceries   Furniture

CHURCH

To be completed for husband and wife

	Husband	Wife
Do you go to church:		
1. Once a month or more?		
2. Less than once a month?		
3. Never (weddings etc.)?		
Where do you go? (Church/Denomination)		
With whom do you go?		
Do you take part in any social activities run by a church?	Yes/No	Yes/No
If yes, please specify		
Where do you go?		
With whom do you go?		

POLITICAL LIFE

We are not interested in your politics

Are you a member of a major political party	Yes/No
Do you belong to the Ratepayers' Association?	Yes/No

Did you vote in the recent

County Council elections?	Yes/No
Parish Council elections?	Yes/No

Do you take part in social activities run by a major political party association?   Yes/No

If yes, please specify

With whom do you go?

COMMUNITY FEELING

What do you like about Maghull?

What do you dislike about Maghull?

Do you feel that you belong to Maghull? (*Comments*)

Do you feel that you have enough privacy? (*Comments*)

What do you think about the provision of the following in Maghull?

(*N.B. N/A, e.g. Schools—people without children*)

Shopping	Social life
Public transport	Entertainment
Primary schools	Hospital treatment
Secondary schools	Clinics
Schoolchildren's leisure	Old people's welfare
Young people's leisure	

Are you satisfied with:

    Maghull/Lydiate Parish Council?

    West Lancs. Rural District Council?

    Lancashire County Council?

Are there any other comments you would like to make?

Index